C A R S

CARS

Sandcastle Books

Published in 2008 by Sandcastle Books Ltd

Orchard House,
6, Butt Furlong
Fladbury
Worcestershire, UK
WR10 2QZ

Produced by TAJ Books International LLP

27, Ferndown Gardens,
Cobham,
Surrey,
UK,
KT11 2BH

www.tajbooks.com

The Publishers wish to thank all of the manufacturers covered in this book for their cooperation in supplying photography.

All notations of errors or omissions (author inquiries, permissions) concerning the content of this book
should be addressed to TAJ Books 27, Ferndown Gardens, Cobham, Surrey, UK, KT11 2BH, info@tajbooks.com.

ISBN-13: 978-1-906536-16-9

Printed in China.

CONTENTS

INTRODUCTION

A Model T Ford

Although Nicolas-Joseph Cugnot is often credited with building the first self-propelled mechanical vehicle or automobile in about 1769, this claim is disputed by some, who doubt Cugnot's three-wheeler ever ran. Others claim Ferdinand Verbiest, a member of a Jesuit mission in China, built the first steam-powered 'car' around 1672. What is not in doubt is that Richard Trevithick built and demonstrated his Puffing Devil road locomotive in 1801, the first truly successful steam-powered road vehicle.

François Isaac de Rivaz, a Swiss inventor, designed the first internal combustion engine, in 1806, which was fuelled by a mixture of hydrogen and oxygen and used it to develop the world's first vehicle to run on such an engine. The design was not very successful, as was the case with Samuel Brown, Samuel Morey, and Etienne Lenoir who each produced vehicles powered by clumsy internal combustion engines.

In November 1881 French inventor Gustave Trouvé demonstrated a working three-wheeled automobile. This was at the International Exhibition of Electricity in Paris.

An automobile powered by an Otto gasoline engine was built in Mannheim, Germany by Karl Benz in 1885 and granted a patent in January of the following year under the auspices of his major company, Benz & Cie. which was founded in 1883.

Although several other German engineers (including Gottlieb Daimler, Wilhelm Maybach, and Siegfried Marcus) were working

on the problem at about the same time, Karl Benz is generally acknowledged as the inventor of the modern automobile. In 1879 Benz was granted a patent for his first engine, designed in 1878. Many of his other inventions made the use of the internal combustion engine feasible for powering a vehicle and in 1896, Benz designed and patented the first internal combustion flat engine.

Approximately 25 Benz vehicles were built and sold before 1893, when his first four-wheeler was introduced. They were powered with four-stroke engines of his own design. Emile Roger of France, already producing Benz engines under license, now added the Benz automobile to his line of products. Because France was more open to the early automobiles, more were built and sold in France through Roger than Benz sold in Germany.

Daimler and Maybach founded Daimler Motoren Gesellschaft (Daimler Motor Company, DMG) in Cannstatt in 1890 and under the brand name, Daimler, sold their first automobile in 1892. By 1895 about 30 vehicles had been built by Daimler and Maybach, either at the Daimler works or in the Hotel Hermann, where they set up shop after falling out with their backers. Benz and Daimler seem to have been unaware of each other's early work and worked independently.

Daimler died in 1900 and later that year, Maybach designed

A 1934 Bentley

a model named Daimler-Mercedes, special-ordered by Emil Jellinek. Two years later, a new model DMG automobile was produced and named Mercedes after the engine. Maybach quit DMG shortly thereafter and opened a business of his own. Rights to the Daimler brand name were sold to other manufacturers.

Karl Benz proposed co-operation between DMG and Benz & Cie. when economic conditions began to deteriorate in Germany following the First World War, but the directors of DMG refused to consider it initially. Negotiations between the two companies resumed several years later and in 1924 they signed an Agreement of Mutual Interest valid until the year 2000. Both enterprises standardized design, production, purchasing, sales, and advertising—marketing their automobile models jointly—although keeping their respective brands. On June 28, 1926, Benz & Cie. and DMG finally merged as the Daimler-Benz company, baptizing all of its automobiles Mercedes Benz honoring the most important model of the DMG automobiles, the Maybach design

later referred to as the 1902 Mercedes-35hp, along with the Benz name. Karl Benz remained a member of the board of directors of Daimler-Benz until his death in 1929.

In 1890, Emile Levassor and Armand Peugeot of France began producing vehicles with Daimler engines, and so laid the foundation of the motor industry in France. The first American car with a gasoline internal combustion engine supposedly was designed in 1877 by George Selden of Rochester, New York, who applied for a patent on an automobile in 1879. In Britain there had been several attempts to build steam cars with varying degrees of success with Thomas Rickett even attempting a production run in 1860. Santler from Malvern is recognized by the Veteran Car Club of Great Britain as having made the first petrol-powered car in the country in 1894 followed by Frederick William Lanchester in 1895 but these were both one-offs. The first production vehicles came from the Daimler Motor Company, founded by Harry J.

INTRODUCTION

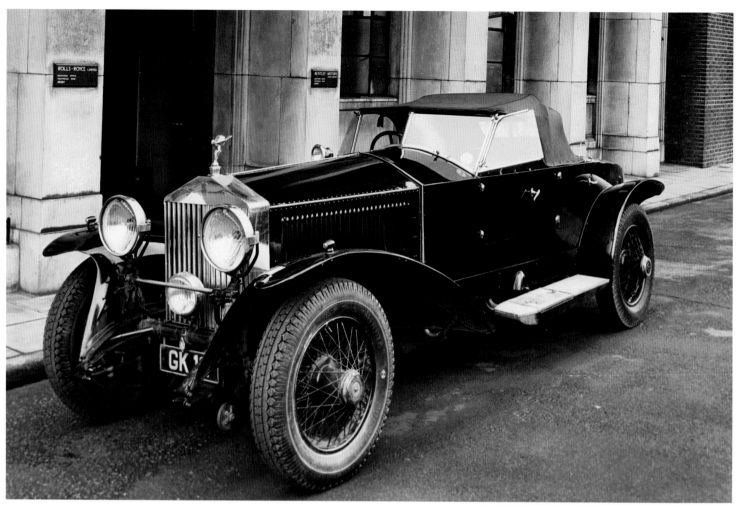

1928 Rolls Royce 16EX

Lawson in 1896, and making their first cars in 1897.

In 1892, German engineer Rudolf Diesel got a patent for a "New Rational Combustion Engine". In 1897 he built the first Diesel Engine. In 1895, Selden was granted a United States patent (U.S. Patent 549,160) for a two-stroke automobile engine, which hindered more than encouraged development of autos in the United States. Steam, electric, and gasoline powered autos competed for decades, with gasoline internal combustion engines achieving dominance in the 1910s.

Although various pistonless rotary engine designs have attempted to compete with the conventional piston and crankshaft design, only Mazda's version of the Wankel engine has had more than very limited success.

Production

The large-scale, production-line manufacturing of affordable automobiles was debuted by Ransom Olds at his Oldsmobile factory in 1902. This concept was then greatly expanded by Henry Ford, beginning in 1914.

As a result, Ford's cars came off the line in fifteen minute intervals, much faster than previous methods, increasing production by seven to one (requiring 12.5 man-hours before, 1 hour 33 minutes after), while using less manpower. It was so successful, paint became a bottleneck. Only Japan black would

dry fast enough, forcing the company to drop the variety of colors available before 1914, until fast-drying Duco lacquer was developed in 1926. In 1914, an assembly line worker could buy a Model T with four months' pay.

Ford's complex safety procedures—especially assigning each worker to a specific location instead of allowing them to roam about—dramatically reduced the rate of injury. The combination of high wages and high efficiency is called "Fordism," and was copied by most major industries. The efficiency gains from the assembly line also coincided with the take off of the United States. The assembly line forced workers to work at a certain pace with very repetitive motions which led to more output per worker while other countries were using less productive methods.

In the automotive industry, its success was dominating, and quickly spread worldwide. Ford France and Ford Britain in 1911, Ford Denmark 1923, Ford Germany 1925; in 1921, Citroen was the first native European manufacturer to adopt it. Soon, companies had to have assembly lines, or risk going broke; by 1930, 250 companies which did not had disappeared.

Development of automotive technology was rapid, due in part to the hundreds of small manufacturers competing to gain the world's attention. Key developments included electric ignition and the electric self-starter (both by Charles Kettering,

1963 Lamborghini 350 GTV

for the Cadillac Motor Company in 1910-1911), independent suspension, and four-wheel brakes.

Since the 1920s, nearly all cars have been mass-produced to meet market needs, so marketing plans have often heavily influenced automobile design. It was Alfred P. Sloan who established the idea of different makes of cars produced by one company, so buyers could "move up" as their fortunes improved.

Reflecting the rapid pace of change, makes shared parts with one another so larger production volume resulted in lower costs for each price range. For example, in the 1930s, LaSalles, sold by Cadillac, used cheaper mechanical parts made by Oldsmobile; in the 1950s, Chevrolet shared hood, doors, roof, and windows with Pontiac; by the 1990s, corporate drivetrains and shared platforms (with interchangeable brakes, suspension, and other parts) were common. Even so, only major makers could afford high costs, and even companies with decades of production, such as Apperson, Cole, Dorris, Haynes, or Premier, could not manage: of some two hundred carmakers in existence in 1920, only 43 survived in 1930, and with the Great Depression, by 1940, only 17 of those were left.

In Europe, much the same would happen. Morris set up its production line at Cowley in 1924, and soon outsold Ford, while beginning in 1923 to follow Ford's practise of vertical integration, buying Hotchkiss (engines), Wrigley (gearboxes), and Osberton

(radiators), for instance, as well as competitors, such as Wolseley: in 1925, Morris had 41% of total British car production. Most British small-car assemblers, from Autocrat to Meteorite to Seabrook, to name only three, had gone under. Germany's first mass-manufactured car, the Opel 4PS Laubfrosch (Tree Frog), came off the line at Russelsheim in 1924, soon making Opel the top car builder in Germany, with 37.5% of the market.

Most automobiles in use today are propelled by gasoline (also known as petrol) or diesel internal combustion engines, which are known to cause air pollution and are also blamed for contributing to climate change and global warming. Increasing costs of oil-based fuels, tightening environmental laws and restrictions on greenhouse gas emissions are propelling work on alternative power systems for automobiles. Efforts to improve or replace existing technologies include the development of hybrid vehicles, and electric and hydrogen vehicles which do not release pollution into the air.

INTRODUCTION

A 1950 Ford Zephyr

Diesel

Diesel-engined cars have long been popular in Europe with the first models being introduced in the 1930s by Mercedes Benz and Citroen. The main benefit of diesel engines is a 50% fuel burn efficiency compared with 27% in the best gasoline engines. A down-side of the diesel is the presence in the exhaust gases of fine soot particulates and manufacturers are now starting to fit filters to remove these. Many diesel-powered cars can also run with little or no modifications on 100% biodiesel.

Gasoline

Gasoline engines have the advantage over diesel in being lighter and able to work at higher rotational speeds and they are the usual choice for fitting in high-performance sports cars. Continuous development of gasoline engines for over a hundred years has produced improvements in efficiency and reduced pollution. The carburetor was used on nearly all road car engines until the 1980s but it was long realised better control of the fuel/air mixture could be achieved with fuel injection. Indirect fuel injection was first used in aircraft engines from 1909, in racing car engines from the 1930s, and road cars from the late 1950s. Gasoline Direct Injection (GDI) is now starting to appear in production vehicles such as the 2007 (Mark II) BMW Mini. Exhaust gases are also cleaned up by fitting a catalytic converter into the exhaust system. Clean air legislation in many of the car industries most important

markets has made both catalysts and fuel injection virtually universal fittings. Most modern gasoline engines are also capable of running with up to 15% ethanol mixed into the gasoline - older vehicles may have seals and hoses that can be harmed by ethanol. With a small amount of redesign, gasoline-powered vehicles can run on ethanol concentrations as high as 85%. 100% ethanol is used in some parts of the world (such as Brazil), but vehicles must be started on pure gasoline and switched over to ethanol once the engine is running. Most gasoline engined cars can also run on LPG with the addition of an LPG tank for fuel storage and carburetion modifications to add an LPG mixer. LPG produces fewer toxic emissions and is a popular fuel for fork lift trucks that have to operate inside buildings.

Bioalcohols and biogasoline

Ethanol, other alcohol fuels (biobutanol) and biogasoline have widespread use an automotive fuel. Most alcohols have less energy per liter than gasoline and are usually blended with gasoline. Alcohols are used for a variety of reasons - to increase octane, to improve emissions, and as an alternative to petroleum based fuel, since they can be made from agricultural crops. Brazil's ethanol program provides about 20% of the nations automotive fuel needs, including several million cars that operate on pure ethanol.

Electric

The first electric cars were built around 1832, well before internal combustion powered cars appeared. For a period of time electrics were considered superior due to the silent nature of electric motors compared to the very loud noise of the gasoline engine. This advantage was removed with Hiram Percy Maxim's invention of the muffler in 1897. Thereafter internal combustion powered cars had two critical advantages: 1) long range and 2) high specific energy (far lower weight of petrol fuel versus weight of batteries). The building of battery electric vehicles that could rival internal combustion models had to wait for the introduction of modern semiconductor controls and improved batteries. Because they can deliver a high torque at low revolutions electric cars do not require such a complex drive train and transmission as internal combustion powered cars. Some post-2000 electric car designs such as the Venturi Fétish are able to accelerate from 0-60 mph (96 km/h) in 4.0 seconds with a top speed around 130 mph (210 km/h). Others have a range of 250 miles (400 km) on the EPA highway cycle requiring 3-1/2 hours to completely charge. Equivalent fuel efficiency to internal combustion is not well defined but some press reports give it at around 135 mpg–U.S. (1.74 L/100 km / 162.1 mpg–imp).

Steam

Steam power, usually using an oil or gas heated boiler, was also in use until the 1930s but had the major disadvantage of being unable to power the car until boiler pressure was available. It has the advantage of being able to produce very low emissions as the combustion process can be carefully controlled. Its disadvantages include poor heat efficiency and extensive requirements for electric auxiliaries.

Gas turbine

In the 1950s there was a brief interest in using gas turbine (jet) engines and several makers including Rover and Chrysler produced prototypes. In spite of the power units being very compact, high fuel consumption, severe delay in throttle response, and lack of engine braking meant no cars reached production.

Rotary (Wankel) engines

Rotary Wankel engines were introduced into road cars by NSU with the Ro 80 and later were seen in the Citroën GS Birotor and several Mazda models. In spite of their impressive smoothness, poor reliability and fuel economy led to them largely disappearing. Mazda, beginning with the R100 then RX-2, has continued research on these engines, overcoming most of the earlier problems with the RX-7 and RX-8.

Rocket and jet cars

A rocket car holds the record in drag racing. However, the fastest of those cars are used to set the Land Speed Record, and are propelled by propulsive jets emitted from rocket, turbojet, or more recently and most successfully turbofan engines. The ThrustSSC car using two Rolls-Royce Spey turbofans with reheat was able to exceed the speed of sound at ground level in 1997.

Future car technologies

Automobile propulsion technology under development include gasoline/electric and plug-in hybrids, battery electric vehicles, hydrogen cars, biofuels, and various alternative fuels.

Research into future alternative forms of power include the development of fuel cells, Homogeneous Charge Compression Ignition (HCCI), stirling engines, and even using the stored energy of compressed air or liquid nitrogen.

New materials which may replace steel car bodies include duraluminum, fiberglass, carbon fiber, and carbon nanotubes.

Telematics technology is allowing more and more people to share cars, on a pay-as-you-go basis, through such schemes as City Car Club in the UK, Mobility in mainland Europe, and Zipcar in the US.

Auto engineers have developed sophisticated emissions-control technology that is putting cleaner automobiles on the road everywhere. Catalytic converters use precious metals to reduce smog-forming emissions from cars. Automakers have dramatically reduced evaporative emissions with tighter gaskets, hoses and better gas tanks. Computers have revolutionized clean vehicle controls by precisely metering the fuel and air that go into the engine, reducing the smog-forming emissions coming out of the engine. And, a computer system called aeon-board diagnostics constantly monitors the performance of the vehicle to help keep clean technology working.

As more and more new cars with modern exhaust emissions performance are put on the road, clear improvements in air quality can be seen. This trend is going to continue, even without the further improvements planned for new vehicles in the future, as older, more polluting cars, which are responsible for a large proportion of all vehicle emissions, are replaced with new ones. In fact, anything which could speed up this process, would make a much greater improvement to air quality than the further reductions in the already very low emissions from new cars, because the effect of that will be quite small, and will take a long time to be effective.

INTRODUCTION

The table below gives the world's largest twenty motor vehicle manufacturing groups, along with their marques, classified as divisions and subsidiary companies.

Marque	Ownership	Markets
1. Toyota Motor Corporation (Japan)		
Daihatsu	Subsidiary	Global, except North America
Hino	Subsidiary	Asia Pacific, Canada, South America
Lexus	Division	Global, except South America, but Chile.
Scion	Division	United States
Toyota	Division	Global
2. General Motors Corporation (United States)		
Buick	Division	North America, China
Cadillac	Division	Global
Chevrolet	Division	Global
Daewoo	Subsidiary	Asia, Europe, South America
GMC	Division	North America, Middle East
Pontiac	Division	North America
Holden	Subsidiary	Asia Pacific, Middle East
Hummer	Division	Global
Opel	Subsidiary	Continental Europe, South Africa
Saturn	Subsidiary	North America
Saab	Subsidiary	Global
Vauxhall	Subsidiary	United Kingdom
3. Ford Motor Company (United States)		
Ford	Division	Global
Lincoln	Division	North America, Middle East
Mercury	Division	North America, Middle East
Volvo Cars	Subsidiary	Global
Troller	Subsidiary	South America
4. Volkswagen AG (Germany)		
Audi	Subsidiary	Global
Bentley	Subsidiary	Global
Bugatti	Subsidiary	Global
Lamborghini	Subsidiary	Global
Scania	Subsidiary	Global
SEAT	Subsidiary	Europe, Latin America, South Africa
Škoda	Subsidiary	Global, except North America
Volkswagen	Division	Global
Volkswagen Commercial Vehicles	Division	Global
5. Honda Motor Company (Japan)		
Acura	Division	North America, China
Honda	Division	Global
6. PSA Peugeot Citroën (France)		
Citroën	Division	Global, except North America
Peugeot	Division	Global, except United States and Canada
7. Nissan Motors (Japan)		
Infiniti	Division	North America, Middle East, Taiwan, Korea, Western Europe
Nissan	Division	Global
8. Chrysler LLC (United States)		
Chrysler	Division	Global

Dodge	Division	Global
Jeep	Division	Global
9. RENAULT S.A. (FRANCE)		
Dacia	Subsidiary	Europe, Latin America, Asia, Africa
Renault	Division	Global, except United States and Canada
Samsung	Subsidiary	Asia, South America
10. HYUNDAI MOTOR COMPANY (SOUTH KOREA)		
Hyundai	Division	Global
11. FIAT S.p.A. (ITALY)		
Abarth	Subsidiary	Global, except United States and Canada
Alfa Romeo	Subsidiary	Global, except United States and Canada
Ferrari	Subsidiary	Global
Fiat	Division	Global, except United States and Canada
Iveco	Subsidiary	Global, except North America
Maserati	Subsidiary	Global
Lancia	Subsidiary	Global, except North America
Zastava	Subsidiary	Global
12. SUZUKI MOTOR CORPORATION (JAPAN)		
Maruti Suzuki	Subsidiary	India, Middle East, South America
Suzuki	Division	Global
13. DAIMLER AG (GERMANY)		
Mercedes-Benz	Division	Global
Mercedes-AMG	Division	Global
Maybach	Division	Global
Smart	Division	Western Europe, Southeast Asia, North America, South Africa
Mitsubishi Fuso	Subsidiary	Global
Freightliner	Subsidiary	North America
14. MAZDA MOTOR CORPORATION (JAPAN)		
Mazda	Division	Global
15. KIA MOTORS (SOUTH KOREA)		
Kia	Division	Global
16. BMW AG (GERMANY)		
BMW	Division	Global
MINI	Division	Global
Rolls-Royce	Subsidiary	Global
17. MITSUBISHI MOTORS CORPORATION (JAPAN)		
Mitsubishi	Division	Global
18. AvtoVAZ (RUSSIA)		
Lada	Division	Russia, Finland, Sweden
VAZ	Division	Russia, Eastern Europe
19. FUJI HEAVY INDUSTRIES (JAPAN)		
Subaru	Division	Global
20. TATA MOTORS LIMITED (INDIA)		
Hispano	Subsidiary	Europe
Jaguar	Subsidiary	Global
Land Rover	Subsidiary	Global
Tata	Subsidiary	Division
Tata Daewoo Commercial Vehicle	Subsidiary	South Korea

INTRODUCTION

This is a list of countries by automobile production in 2007 based on OICA accessed in April 2008.

RANK BY SOVEREIGN STATE	COUNTRY/REGION	AUTOMOBILE PRODUCTION
	World	73,101,695
	EU	18,887,996
1	Japan	11,596,327
2	US	10,780,729
3	People's Republic of China	8,882,456
4	Germany	6,213,460
5	South Korea	4,086,308
6	France	3,019,144
7	Brazil	2,970,818
8	Spain	2,889,703
9	Canada	2,578,238
10	India	2,306,768
11	Mexico	2,095,245
12	United Kingdom	1,750,253
13	Russia	1,660,120
14	Italy	1,284,312
15	Thailand	1,238,460
16	Turkey	1,099,414
17	Iran	997,240
18	Czech Republic	938,527
19	Belgium	844,030
20	Poland	784,700
21	Slovakia	571,071
22	Argentina	544,647
23	South Africa	534,490
24	Indonesia	419,040
25	Malaysia	413,440
26	Ukraine	402,591
27	Sweden	366,020
28	Australia	334,617

RANK BY SOVEREIGN STATE	COUNTRY/REGION	AUTOMOBILE PRODUCTION
29	Hungary	292,027
30	Taiwan	283,039
31	Romania	241,712
32	Austria	228,066
33	Slovenia	198,402
34	Portugal	176,242
35	Venezuela	172,418
35	Pakistan	162,000
35	Netherlands	138,568
36	Uzbekistan	135,400
39	Egypt	103,140
40	Colombia	73,467
38	Philippines	42,000
43	Morocco	36,023
45	Ecuador	25,170
42	Finland	24,303
46	Belarus	23,150
44	Vietnam	20,750
48	Serbia	9,903
49	Chile	5,685
50	Nigeria	3,000
51	Zimbabwe	1,420
52	Kenya	600

►The Hydrogen Fuel-cell powered Chevrolet Volt

The Citroën C2 is a supermini produced by the French manufacturer Citroën since 2003. A completely different car, based on the Peugeot 206, is sold in China as the C2.

Along with the Citroën C3, the C2 was intended to replace the popular Citroën Saxo. The two cars have relatively different designs allowing Citroën to grab different sub-markets of the supermini class. The C2 was designed by Donato Coco. The C3 was originally designed as a larger "family friendly" vehicle" being 5 doors, whereas the C2 is seen as a "young driver" image with 2 doors and flatter styling, though still with low power.

The L model is the "no-frills" version of the C2 and comes with basic equipment, including black plastic bumpers and no fog lamps. The LX model, produced from 2003 to 2005, came with black lower bumper and door handles, CD player, rear seat modulation and no fog lamps. The Design includes body-coloured bumpers and electric windows. The SX is the luxury spec. It features 'bumper colour coded paint' and air conditioning, the latter of which has an unfortunate effect on the 1.1 SX performance, increasing the 0-100 km/h time by 3 seconds to 17.2 seconds.

The Furio, VTR and VTS are the sports models which made the C2's predecessor, the Saxo, famous as an affordable, sporty-looking and very fast 'pocket rocket'. The Furio has exactly the same sports body kit as the more expensive VTR and VTS models but lacks the alloy wheels of those models.

The VTR also has an adequate 110 bhp engine, whereas the VTS is the premium sports model, with a 125 bhp engine capable of accelerating from 0 to 60 mph in 8.2 seconds, seen as sluggish by modern hot hatch standards where the fastest hot hatch achieves 5.3 seconds (Clio V6), although this is obviously designed to be more insurance-friendly. Other additions which helped the VTS model achieve a low insurance rating were security based including deadlocks and a Thatcham Category 1 alarm system which includes perimeter and volumetric detection as well as engine immobiliser.

2004's limited edition GT model offered a sporty bodykit, with bright red, blue, silver and black paintwork and unique white alloy wheels. All GTs had a number certificate to show their authenticity.

2006 saw a number of revisions to the C2. Externally the car looks identical save minor changes to alloy wheels (on the VTR), clear side indicator lenses, and white indicator rear lenses. Internal changes saw a new electrical system, new stereo with vehicle computer integration and some cosmetic changes to the driver displays.

DAIHATSU *Materia*

The Daihatsu Materia is a mini MPV manufactured by the Japanese automaker Daihatsu. It is based on the platform of the second generation of the Daihatsu Sirion and is largely identical to the second generation of the Toyota bB.

Comes in 1.3L and 1.5L varieties with a 4WD version in the pipeline, manual and Auto versions. (Currently in UK they only have the 1.5L Version 16/11/2007) 0-60 mph times 10.8 seconds for manual, and 13.7 seconds for Auto (UK Versions).

Maximum speed of 106 mph (171 km/h) and for automatic 102 mph (164 km/h).

Fiat previewed the all new 500 in March 2007 exactly 50 years after the first Fiat 500 was presented.

The design of the new 2007 Fiat 500 is based on the 2004 Fiat Trepiuno concept. This car will feature a distinctive retro-look just like the Volkswagen New Beetle and BMW MINI but may well be substantially cheaper than those cars. The car is 3.55 meters long and 1.65 meters wide. Top speed is 180 km/h (112 mph). The basic price is 10,500 euro in Italy; with options 15,000 euro.

Fiat will share the underpinnings of the new 500 with Ford for the next Ford Ka. Production took place in Fiat facilities in Poland, in 2007 with the commercial debut in September of 2007.

Three engines are available. A 1.2 8v unit, the 75 bhp 1.3 Multijet common-rail turbo diesel, and a 85 bhp 1.4 16v engine coupled to a 6 speed manual gearbox as found in the Panda 100HP. Currently, three trims are available the Pop, Sport and Lounge. A fourth more basic model called 'Naked' may be put on sale, although it is doubted whether it will be available in all markets.

A Fiat 500 Abarth will be unveiled at the 2008 Geneva Motor Show, and it will be powered by a 1.4 liter Fire engine with an IHI variable geometry turbocharger. The Abarth will have 135 horsepower and 180Nm of torque, with the option for 206Nm in sports mode.

The all-new 500 received critical acclaim from many magazines. British-magazine Car called the new Fiat "irresistible". The car also received a full five star EURO NCAP crash test rating.

The Ford Focus is a small family car made by Ford and sold in most Ford markets worldwide. It was launched in 1998 in Europe and 2002 in Australia. Since then, it has become the United Kingdom's best selling car, following in the success of its predecessor, the Escort. In 2001 and 2002, the Focus was the world's best selling car. A new version of the Focus was launched in Europe in January 2005 and a face lifted version in January 2008.

In Europe, South America and South Africa, the Focus replaced the Ford Escort. In Australia, New Zealand, and Japan, it replaced the Ford Laser.

Codenamed CW170 during its development, and briefly known to some Ford contractors as the Ford Fusion , the original Focus took its eventual name from a Ghia concept car which was shown at the Geneva Motor Show in 1991. Certain elements of the design had been seen even earlier in prototypes used by Ford to demonstrate forthcoming safety features, such as the eye-level rear lighting clusters. Initial spy photographs of the car seen in 1995 showed a continuation of Ford's New Edge styling philosophy, first seen in the Ford Ka in 1996, and Ford Cougar in 1998.

The decision to call the new car the Ford Focus was made in early 1998, as Ford's overheads had been planning to keep the Escort nameplate for its new generation of small family cars.

The interior of the car was also radically styled featuring many curves and sweeping lines. Although the design was clearly influenced by the Ka the interior design was more akin to those of American cars, in the same way the original Mondeo was.

The Focus also introduced high specification components. The car featured a highly sophisticated fully independent multi-link rear suspension (dubbed "Control Blade") which was derived from the system used on the Ford Mondeo estate and was intended to give the car class-leading handling and ride. Although fully independent multi-link rear suspension is costly, Ford managed to design and produce the suspension in an ingenious and cost effective way by using pressed metal techniques. Until then a high proportion of other cars in the class had used Twist-beam rear suspensions , or other beam type suspensions.

Ford unveiled a facelifted Mk2 Ford Focus at the Frankfurt Motor Show in September 2007, to go on sale in early 2008 in the hatchback, estate and saloon bodystyles, with the Coupé-Cabriolet and ST to follow in Spring 2008, it went on sale in the UK on 2nd Feb 2008.

In November 2007, the BBC reported Sheffield University survey data as showing that 40% of UK families owned two cars, and one was was 'likely to be a Focus'.

The Focus was Britain's best selling car once again for 2007 - the ninth successive year that it has achieved this success. It is now just one year away from achieving the Ford Cortina's record of ten successive years as Britain's best selling car.

HONDA *Fit*

The Honda Fit is a five-door hatchback automobile produced by Honda of Japan, that was first introduced in June 2001. The vehicle is known as the Fit in Japan, China, and in both North and South America. It is called the Jazz in Europe, some parts of Asia, Australia, Oceania, the Middle East, and Africa.

Although the Honda Fit is now one of Honda's global models, it experienced a very slow progression as it made its way around the world. The car first debuted in the June of 2001 in Japan and immediately became a big hit. It was then introduced to Europe (early 2002), Australia (late 2002), South America (early 2003), South Africa and South-East Asia (mid 2003), China (mid 2004), and Mexico (late 2005). A production model for the United States and Canadian markets debuted on January 8, 2006 at the North American International Auto Show in Detroit. The car was released in Canada on April 3, 2006, and in the U.S. on April 20, 2006.

On 17 July 2007, Honda CEO, Takeo Fukui, announced during a press event that the next-generation Honda Fit/Jazz would make its debut in the fall of 2007 in Japan. Events leading up to the introduction of the second-generation Honda Fit slowly unveiled more information about the vehicle. On 28 August, 2007, manufacturer brochures were leaked and indicated that the second generation Honda Fit may feature three trim levels; G, L and RS. It is speculated the G and L trim levels will feature a new 1.3 L (79.3 cu in) i-VTEC engine that makes 98 hp (73 kW), while the 1.5 L (91.5 cu in) i-VTEC will be reserved for the Fit RS and will feature 118 hp (88 kW).

On 20 August, 2007, Honda released official pictures and specifications of the new Fit. The vehicle was wider, longer, and with a longer wheelbase. Height was unchanged due to mechanic parking in Japan. ULTR magic seats were retained in the second generation, rear headrests were redesigned for better convenience when folding down the seats which now only takes two steps to fold down the whole back row. Growth in dimensions brought more space to the cabin, boot capacity increased from 12.7 to 14.2 cubic feet (0.40 m³). There is also a hidden box under the floor. Although there is no increase in the height of the body, the interior height gained another .3 in, being benefited by the new layout of the platform.

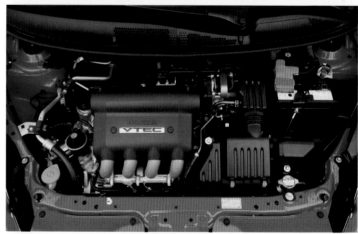

Two engines will be offered in the new Fit. A 1.3 L (79.3 cu in) i-VTEC will produce 98 hp (73 kW) at 6000 rpm and 98 lb·ft (133 N·m) at 4500 rpm. This engine will be offered in both European and Asian markets. A 1.5 L (91.5 cu in) i-VTEC engine will also be offered and have a maximum output of 118 hp (88 kW) at 6000 rpm and 107 lb·ft (145 N·m) at 4800 rpm. This will be the only engine available in the American market. A 5-speed manual, 5-speed automatic (4WD only) and CVT transmission are available.

The chassis was thoroughly reengineered and improvements have improved structural rigidity by 164 percent.

In the 1980s Ford approached Mazda to create a B-segment small car for it. This resulted in the 1987 Ford Festiva. The same platform spawned the Autozam Revue in 1990, which Mazda sold as the 121 in most markets. Then the Festiva was redesigned in January 1993, still based on the same platform. Kia also built versions of the first and second Festiva, both for itself and for Ford's sale in the United States (Kia Pride and Kia Avella).

The new Mazda2 is the first of Mazda's Zoom-Zoom cars to receive an upgrade. The new Mazda2 is also a radical departure from the 2002 model. It abandons the practical and boxy shape and replaces it with a more sleek body. The Demio is expected to be revamped for the 2007 model year, with the sporty MicroSport coupe added for Europe and Japan.

The all new 2 is built on an all new automobile platform, shared with the upcoming 2008 Ford Fiesta. It deploys light weight material and reduces the overall dimensions of the car; this was due to enhanced development opportunities. A new 1.3 litre and a new 1.5 litre engines were introduced these engines will be coupled with a five speed manual or a four speed automatic. Inside the vehicle major improvements are apparent, with the adoption of MX-5 styled air vents and dashboard qualities.

A digital fuel gauge had been introduced to improve fuel monitoring equipment. Stability control will not be standard in the Mazda 2 range but is available as a $1000 extra. The suspension and NVH levels have been improved to help vehicle quality. In an Australian fuel cycle the 2 can achieve 6 litres/100km which is average for this type of car. There are two trim levels available for the new 2 range, the first is known as the Neo which is the base model. It comes standard with air-conditioning and 15-inch alloy wheels, though side air bags, 16-inch alloy wheels and a sports body kit come as standard on the range topping Genki.

Mazda has announced that the next generation of the car, referred to as "the next sub compact, B-segment Mazda", will not be manufactured in Valencia, Spain, but in Hiroshima, Japan . It will feature either an MZR 1.35 liter engine, or a larger MZR 1.5 liter engine. Additionally, Mazda has released information regarding a Mazda2 MPS model with a direct-injection Turbo engine and all-wheel-drive. Photos of the new Mazda2 can be seen in Mazda's pertinent press release.

Mazda has already announced that the sedan verion of Mazda2 will be produced for the Chinese market by Changan Ford Mazda Automobile Co., Ltd. at its Nanjing plant. The car will go on sale in the first half of 2008 .

From November 2006, the hatchback MINI range has been replaced by an all-new MINI, consisting of MINI Cooper and MINI Cooper S models, powered by a new 1.6 litre engine co-developed by BMW and PSA Peugeot-Citroën. The "old" MINI Convertible continues to be sold alongside the new hatchback range. The Mk II MINI One went on sale in April 2007 with Mk II Convertibles for the 2009 model year. The MINI One has a 1.4 litre engine derived from the same engine in the MINI Cooper and Peugeot 207.

The later "Mk II" MINI (or R56) uses the BMW-PSA 1.4/1.6 Prince 4 cylinder engine. The naturally-aspirated (non-turbo) versions of this engine use a system known as Valvetronic to control valves for optimum performance and/or efficiency. This MINI uses a drivetrain architecture based on that of the Peugeot 207 and the second generation Citroën C3.

The R56 Cooper S boasts direct injection and a twin scroll turbocharger featuring an overboost function for added torque. This engine produces 128 kW (175 HP) and 240 N·m (177 ft·lbf) of torque. The Overboost function momentarily increases torque to 260 Nm (192 ft·lbf)

The new Cooper D model is available from April 2007, featuring a 1.6 litre, 16-valve turbodiesel engine producing 80 kW (110 HP) and 240 N·m (177 ft·lbf) of torque. This unit also features the overboost function momentarily increases torque to 260 N·m (192 ft·lbf)

Technical innovations include an electrically driven power steering system that avoids taking power directly from the engine, equal length driveshafts to eliminate torque steer, and a sophisticated multi-link rear suspension usually found only on rear wheel drive cars. The Mini has a 'drive by wire' electronic throttle, electronic brakeforce distribution, cornering brake control, and electronic stability control to improve control and handling in adverse conditions.

With the introduction of the R56 MINI, the CVT transmission has been dispensed with altogether, and replaced by an hydraulic automatic transmission unit, similar to that of the previous Cooper S. This gearbox is available throughout the whole range of R56 Minis, appearing lastly on the Cooper D from 2008. Additionally, steering-wheel mounted paddle-shift is also available.

The MINI Clubman is a separate model available in Cooper, Cooper D, and Cooper S variations. It is 9.5 in (241 mm) longer to accommodate more leg room and a larger boot. It has double doors as a boot instead of a pull-up hatch. It also features a Club Door on the right-hand side for passengers in the back.

The use of the name 'Clubman' for the MINI estate van is a break with classic Mini tradition. It was originally the name given to the 1970s facelift of the MINI which mostly resulted in a squarer front end. The classic Mini estates were named either 'Traveller' or 'Countryman'. However, BMW did not purchase the rights to use those names.

The Twingo was designed under Patrick le Quément, Renault's chief designer. Le Quément's belief was that it was a greater risk for Renault to take no risks at all, having seen its market share suffer from cars such as the Renault 9 and 11. The design of the Twingo resembles that of the 1982 Polish prototype Beskid (car), from which its monobox silhouette is claimed to be derived.

The Twingo has been built since its launch in France in 1992 and in Colombia and Uruguay from 1999 to 2002, undergoing three intermediate restylings in 1998, 2000 and 2004.

Production of the first generation model ceased at the Flins factory in France on 28th June 2007. It is, however, still produced in Colombia by the Sofasa conglomerate for the South American market. Total production up to 30th June 2007 was 2,478,648.

The Twingo featured revolutionary features (at the time of launch) of a centrally-mounted instrument panel, consisting of a speedometer, fuel gauge and clock, with the odometer and trip recorder selected by pushing a button on the end of the steering column stalk. This left just a strip of warning lights in the area behind the steering wheel. It also had a sliding rear seat, which could be moved to either increase boot space or rear seat legroom. The boot parcel shelf was also unusual in that it was attached to the inside of the tailgate, and lifted up with the tailgate. It could also be clipped back against the rear window when not required.

All the first-generation Twingos were equipped with straight-4 petrol engines. Initially available with an 8-valve 1.2-litre 55 hp (41 kW) engine, it was replaced with an 8-valve 1.1-litre 60 hp (45 kW) unit. A 16-valve 75 hp (56 kW) version was added in 2000. Many parts (e.g. the JB1 gearbox, brakes, engine) are shared with other vehicles across the Renault range.

When the car was launched, Renault's senior bosses said that the British market would not want a city car, so Renault did not produce a right-hand drive version. They were also concerned that it would take away sales from the recently launched Clio, as well as another claim that it would cost too much to engineer the car to right hand specification to make the car competitively priced. Later entrants to this market and their popularity in the United Kingdom, like the Fiat Cinquecento, Ford Ka and Smart Fortwo, suggest that this decision was a mistake. However, many LHD Twingos have been imported from mainland Europe by customers, and all Renault dealers are able to provide servicing and parts for the vehicle.

The Ibiza spans four generations and is still in production. It has been available in either three- or five-door hatchback variants; saloon, coupé and estate versions are sold as the SEAT Córdoba.

The Ibiza Mk I (codenamed 021A) was based on the Fiat 127/ Ritmo/Regata, and used a powertrain which had been developed in collaboration with Porsche. This was the first SEAT which did not share any external body panels with any Fiat model, having been designed by Giorgetto Giugiaro. This version, while it established the now classic Ibiza shape, was advertised as having "Italian styling and German engines".

In terms of size, it was larger than most superminis like the Ford Fiesta and Fiat Uno, but smaller than any small family car such as the Ford Escort and Volkswagen Golf. Styling was fairly imaginative and interior space was good, but the Ibiza was let down by suspect build quality, heavy steering and doubtful reliability.

In the UK, sales couldn't hope to compete with Ford, Vauxhall and Rover (or even imported brands like Volkswagen and Fiat), but the car sold well among buyers who were more interested in budget buys from the likes of Hyundai and Skoda. The Ibiza's moderate sales success gave the marque a decent platform to build on as it looked to increase sales throughout the 1990s.

In 1999 the design was bought by Chinese automaker Nanjing and was redeveloped into the Nanjing Yuejin Soyat.

The Ibiza Mk III (codenamed 6L and sometimes referred to in the United Kingdom as the Mk IV) is the third model to be produced under Volkswagen Group management and is a much more focused car. Built on the same PQ24 platform as the Type 9N Polo, it is intended to have a sporty, performance image and was styled by the Italian designer Walter de'Silva. The model line up includes two hot hatch variants, the Ibiza FR and Cupra. These compensate for the lack of Polo hot hatch variants (the Polo GTI wasn't launched until 2006).

The more aggressive styling has boosted this model ahead of the family-friendly styling of the Polo. It is also the largest Ibiza to date, with room for five adults, and a spacious, if rather short, boot. The standard trim level on this model is noticeably higher than previous models.

This is regarded by some magazines to be the best supermini, with What Car? magazine calling it their best supermini for three years in a row.

The 2006 model made slight aesthetic changes to both the interior and exterior, but keeping it very similar to the 2002 original model. It also introduced engines with increased power (1.2 16V and 1.4 16V) and a new 1.4 litre TDI diesel version. The sport and FR TDI versions use a Pumpe-Düse Diesel engine.

VAUXHALL *Agila*

The first-generation Agila was a rebadged version of the Suzuki Wagon R+, which was produced in Japan. The Agila's Opel-sourced 1.0 and 1.2-litre petrol engines were smaller than the European-market 1.3-litre found in the European-market Wagon R+, but were more powerful and refined. Equipment levels, low asking prices and running costs also contributed towards the Agila's success.

The Agila was built at a General Motors factory in Gliwice, Poland. The Suzuki Wagon R+ was built at the Suzuki plant in Esztergom, Hungary until 2004, and since January 2005 has also been built in Poland.

While many city cars such as the Ford Ka, Volkswagen Lupo, Fiat Seicento and Renault Twingo come with just three doors, the Agila came with five. It was as tall as Korean city cars such as the Hyundai Atos and Kia Picanto.

The second-generation Agila was officially announced on May 15, 2007, and was presented at the 2007 Frankfurt Motor Show. Suzuki sells this model as the Splash. The car is 200 mm (7.9 in) longer than its predecessor, that is bigger than traditional city cars and similar to small superminis and mini MPVs like the Peugeot 1007, Toyota Yaris, Renault Modus and Nissan Micra.

Petrol engines are a three cylinder 1.0-litre 65 hp (48 kW) and a four cylinder 1.2-litre 86 hp (64 kW), and the diesel unit a four cylinder 1.3-litre 75 hp (56 kW) with common rail technology.

The Volvo C30 is a compact car produced by the Volvo division of Ford Motor Company. The C30 is a three-door, four-seat hatchback powered by straight-4 and straight-5 engines. Despite the name, the car is the hatchback / coupe version of the S40/V50/C70 range and therefore uses the same Ford C1 platform as the Ford Focus and Mazda3.

The production car was officially unveiled at the 2006 Paris Motor Show. In mid-2006, the C30 was approved for production launch in late 2006 in Europe. The C30 went on sale in Canada in March 2007 as a 2007 model, and in October 2007 in the United States as a 2008 model, with the T5 as the single version. It is being marketed as a premium hatchback specially designed for first-time Volvo buyers and the youth market. Production is expected to be 65,000 units a year, 75% for sale in the European market.

Notably, the design of the C30 recalls another important Volvo, the 1800ES, the estate adaptation of the P1800 Coupe. According to Simon Lamarre, chief studio designer, "the 1800ES has become one of the icons for Volvo," inspiring the design of the Volvo C30.

The C30 is offered with a wide variety of petrol and diesel engines. Petrol engines include a 100 hp 1.6 litre I4, a 125 hp 1.8 litre I4, a 145 hp 2.0 litre I4, a 170 hp 2.4 liter inline-5, and a 227 hp turbocharged 2.5 litre inline-5. Diesel engines will be a 109 hp 1.6 litre inline-4, a 136 hp 2.0 litre inline-4, and a 180 hp 2.4 litre inline-5. All models will be fitted with a manual gearbox, and the inline-5 petrol versions will have automatic transmissions as an option. Speculation suggesting that a 1.4 litre inline-4 petrol engine from the Ford Focus would be offered proved false and the smallest engine in the range will is the 1.6 litre engines.

The 2008 model year brings some minor changes, mostly adapting the interior to the facelifted S40/V50 and including as standard an Aux audio socket. Only the T5 2.5 litre turbocharged gasoline engine is available in the United States, for both manual and automatic transmissions.

Volvo is developing a plug-in hybrid electric version of the C30 at their California development centre. A concept of the C30 hybrid called the ReCharge was shown in September 2007 at the Frankfurt auto show. The hybrid C30 will be a flex-fuel or diesel-electric hybrid with a powertrain design similar to General Motors' E-Flex platform and its Chevrolet Volt concept vehicle. That is, it will use a series-hybrid design in which the vehicle is driven directly by electric motors powered by a lithium-ion battery pack. A small internal combustion engine will have no direct connection to the drivetrain, but will function only as a backup generator when necessary to recharge the batteries. The C30 hybrid will have a range of approximately 100 kilometres (62 mi) on battery power alone, and will recharge from a standard home electrical outlet in about three hours.

The Audi A3 is an entry-level luxury car/small family car produced by the German automaker Audi since 1996. Two generations of A3 exist, both based on the Volkswagen A platform, which they share with several other models such as the Audi TT, Volkswagen Golf, Caddy and Touran as well as Škoda Octavia and SEAT León.

In the 2003 Geneva Motor Show, Audi launched the second-generation of the A3, the Typ 8P, designed by Walter de'Silva. Originally launched as a three-door hatchback only with four cylinder engines, it featured a new mechanical platform (the PQ35 platform), a redesigned and more spacious interior, new petrol engines with Fuel Stratified Injection and standard six-speed gearboxes (except on the base 1.6).

In mid 2003, the line was updated with two sports models, a 2.0 Turbo FSI version with 200 PS (147 kW) and a 3.2 VR6 engine (for the first time) with 250 PS (184 kW). Quattro four wheel drive and the S-Tronic semi-auto gearbox were introduced as optionals (quattro is standard on the V6) on every model 140 PS (138 hp/103 kW) and over.

A new five-door body, dubbed Sportback, was introduced in June 2004. Unlike the previous generation, the new A3 Sportback is 8 cm (3 in) longer than the base three-door body, and includes improved rear cabin space and a larger luggage compartment (370 litres). It also received the new front grille originally introduced in the A8 W12.

In 2005, the S-Line trim level, with new sporty decorative elements, became available in certain models, and the 3-door received the same frontend as the Sportback. For the first time, the A3 became available in the North American market, exclusively with the Sportback body, with the base 2.0 TFSI introduced in 2005 and the 3.2 V6 quattro following in 2006. In the Spring of 2005, Audi began a massive alternate reality game to advertise for the A3, known as The Art of the Heist.

In April 2006, the lineup was expanded with the introduction of a more powerful 2.0 TDI with 170 PS (125 kW). In August 2006, Audi announced the arrival of the S3 version, which became the new range topper. The 2.0 TFSI engine was uprated to 265 PS (195 kW), thanks to a higher turbo pressure of 1.2 bar, and is available with a standard 6-speed manual and Quattro. The second generation S3 is capable of accelerating to 100 km/h (62 mph) in 5.7 seconds. The springs and dampers were tuned for a harder setting, and ride height lowered by 25 mm (1 inch). 225/40 R18 tyres are standard.

In January 2007, the normally aspirated 2.0 FSI was replaced by a new turbocharged 1.8 TFSI engine, with 160 PS (118 kW).

In the fall of 2007, Audi will introduce a new 1.4L TFSI engine for the A3 and a new "e"-model . The "e"-models, Audi's equivalent of Volkswagen's Blue Motion, is available with the 1.9L TDI engine, and offers a more ecological car, with a CO_2 emission below 120 g/km.

Audi introduced a heavily revised A4 in late 2004, with the internal designation of B7. However, this new range A4 still utilised the existing Volkswagen B6 (PL46) platform, a chassis derived from the outgoing B6, but enjoyed heavily revised steering settings, suspension geometry, new engine ranges, navigation systems and chassis electronics (a new advanced Bosch 8.0 ESP system). Audi's internal platform nomenclature uses PL46 (longitudinal passenger car platform, size 4, generation 6) for both B6 and B7 chassis. The Typ 8E and 8H internal designations are also unchanged from the B6 A4.

The engine lineup received many additions. The 2005 introduction of Fuel Stratified Injection (FSI) on the 2.0 TFSI and 3.2 V6 FSI petrol/gasoline engines, as well as other refinements, increased power output to 200 and 255 PS (147 and 188 kW), respectively. These engines both implement a four-valve per cylinder design. The prior 5-valve design was incompatible with the FSI direct injection system. The 2.0 TDI diesel engine now combines Pumpe Düse (PD) technology with 16 valves for the first time, while the larger 2.5 TDI was increased to 3.0 L, offering 204 PS (150 kW). quattro four-wheel drive remained available on most A4 models. Audi retired its 5-speed manual transmissions in favor of a 6-speed. As before, Multitronic transmission is available on front-wheel drive models, while a 6-speed Tiptronic transmission is available on quattro four-wheel drive models.

In addition to the higher-performance S4 (S for Sport), which carried over the powertrain of the B6 S4, Audi has reintroduced the ultra-high performance RS4 (RS for RennSport) to the lineup, for the first time on the saloon/sedan and Cabriolet body and with a normally aspirated 4.2 V8 FSI engine. Another notable inclusion is the 3rd-generation quattro system which uses a 'default' asymmetric 40:60 front-rear torque distribution (this new asymmetric centre differential was only available initially on the RS4, and later, on the S4. The remainder of the A4 range still utilised the 50:50 split diff). A limited edition variant first introduced in late 2005, named "DTM Edition", was reintroduced in 2006 as a regular option, the 2.0T FSI engine now engineered to 220 PS (162 kW) with standard quattro. The front grill assembly has changed to be a tall trapezoidal shape in the same manner as the C6 (third-generation) Audi A6.

The B7 Cabriolet model arrived later than the other two body variants, with sales beginning in February 2006. Brand new on the Cabriolet was an entry-level 2.0 TDI version, but to date this is not being offered with the Multitronic gearbox.

The Audi A4 offers many safety features, including side airbags, anti-lock brakes (ABS), Electronic Stabilization Programme, and its optional quattro four-wheel drive. It also received the IIHS "Top Safety Pick For 2007"

The 1 Series was first offered to the market in 2004 as a five-door hatchback and is the only rear-wheel drive in its class. It replaced the BMW 3 Series Compact range and is currently the smallest and most affordable vehicle (depending on the engine model) in the BMW range. Unlike its predecessor, the new vehicle is built on its own platform (E87); however, it shares many components with the E90 3 Series. Shared parts include MacPherson struts in the front of the car and a trapezoidal-link rear axle. BMW has stated that it shares over 60% of components with the current E90 BMW 3 Series.

The 1 Series is built in Regensburg and Leipzig, Germany, with the 4 cylinder petrol/gas engines coming from the Hams Hall plant in Coleshill north east of Birmingham, England.

During its first full year on the market in 2005, it became one of BMW's most successful products. 149,493 units were sold, leading to a third-place finish in total numbers sold by model. Only the 3 and 5 Series sold better.

For the 2008 MY, the coupe (code named E82) and coupe convertible (code named E88) variant have been introduced by BMW. U.S. introduction is scheduled for second quarter of 2008.

BMW upgraded the 1 Series for 2007 and introduced a 3-door sports hatch variant (code named E81). Changes to the model were minor headlight and taillight revisions, new front/rear bumpers and minor revisions to the interior. The dashboard has been updated, and a recommended gear indicator is now present on models with manual transmissions.

New technologies include auto start/stop, Brake Energy Regeneration, Electric Power Steering, an electric water pump, and a host of drivetrain modifications designed for fuel economy, increased performance, and lower emissions. BMW marketing has named this combination of technologies EfficientDynamics, which will also be implemented in other BMW models.

The 1 Series is effectively the first in the world to have mild hybrid technology as standard equipment, although BMW is careful in its marketing not to label it as a hybrid vehicle, as this brings market expectation of electrically assisted drive.

The engines available for E81 and E87 are basically the same as found in the E90/E91, with exception for the 3.0 L inline-6, which is slightly modified to produce more power. For the 2008 model year, the 135i is powered by a twin-turbocharged 3.0-liter inline six-cylinder engine that produces 300 horsepower (220 kW) and 300 ft·lbf (410 N·m) of torque from 1,400 rpm. For the 135i Coupe, acceleration from 0–62 mph (0–100 km/h) is 5.3 seconds, and top speed is electronically limited to 155 mph (250 km/h). Fuel efficiency is increased to 30.7 mpg (US) (7.66 L/100 km/36.9 mpg imp), an increase of 18% compared to its predecessor.

The fourth generation BMW M3 was announced on the 2007 Geneva Auto Show (Switzerland, March 6th-18th 2007) with the BMW M3 concept. As was the case with the E46 M3 Concept and E60 M5 Concept, the M3 Concept hid almost nothing of the looks of the production version, that had its world premiere on the 2007 Frankfurt Auto Show IAA (Germany, September 13th to 23rd).

Just as the previous M3 generations all introduced a completely new engine, the fourth generation M3 did the same: the BMW S65 engine was introduced. This S65B40 is a naturally aspirated, high revving 4-litre V8 (based on the S85B50 5-litre V10 that powers the E60/E61 M5 and the E63/E64 M6 to date) delivers 420 DIN-hp (309 kW, 414 SAE-hp) at 8,300 rpm and peak torque is 400 Nm (295 ft·lbf) at 3,900 rpm, which represents a power increase of 22% over the E46 M3. The engine weighs 15 kgs (33 lbs) less than the outgoing six cylinder for a total weight of 202 kg (445 lbs). A six-speed manual transmission is standard. As from April 2008, BMW offers a new double-clutch gearbox, called M-DKG (Doppel-Kupplungs-Getriebe) or M-DCT (Double Clutch Transmission) as an option, which reduces shift pauses to less than a tenth of a second and shortens the car's 0-100 kp/h sprint time by 0.2 seconds vs. the SMG. It features both automatic and manual modes in a manner similar to the SMG gearboxes in the E36 and E46.

The fourth generation M3 is made in 3 different body shapes: the E90 M3 saloon, the E92 M3 coupe and the E93 M3 convertible.

A E91 M3 touring model is due in the first quarter of 2009. A E92 M3 CSL lightweight version is heavily debated and longed for amongst car enthousiasts, and cars suspected to be M3 CSL have already been spotted at the famous Nordschleife (North Loop) of the German Nürburgring.

CHRYSLER *Grand Voyager*

The first generation North American Chrysler Voyager was simply a rebranded Plymouth Voyager, and only appeared due to the termination of the Plymouth nameplate.

The European Chrysler Voyager was first released in 1988, nearly identical to its American counterpart, the Plymouth Voyager; the only differences between the two were the head/taillights and grille. It is still produced today, at Magna Steyr in Austria. Also, modern European Voyagers have different engines, including diesel engines, which are popular in Europe.

Though the Chrysler Voyager is no longer available in North America, it is currently sold in Mexico. The third-gen Voyager sold there was a Dodge Caravan with Chrysler's logos, later, in the fourth-gen was an identical to the North American Voyager, now the Voyager was dropped for a cheapest trim of the Town & Country.

For the fourth generation (of the minivan) in 2001, the Plymouth Voyager was rebadged as the Chrysler Voyager in the US. It was offered in the short wheelbase only. The Chrysler Voyager became the short wheelbase Town and Country for 2004.

The MkI version of the Chrysler Voyager was never a popular car in Europe but when the MkII or Town and Country replaced it in 2001 the car took off in Europe. The only problem with the vehicle is that the diesel versions were sluggish and underpowered and the petrols were very thirsty. The Grand Voyager was only about 2 more inches longer than the Voyager but it had a good-sized boot even when all 7 seats were used. Another appeal for car buyers were the sliding doors (great in car parks) and the privacy windows which most people carriers didn't have.

The MkII still had the same design as the MkI but it had a major improvement: the engine range. The diesel engines were larger and more economical and the petrol engines were more fuel-efficient.

According to EuroNCAP crash test results, the 1996 model Chrysler Voyager 'did so badly in the frontal impact that it earned no points, making it the worst of the group by some margin. The body structure became unstable and the steering column was driven back into the driver's chest and head'. Worse still, the 2006 model Chrysler Voyager faired little better, achieving just 19% in the frontal impact test, with an overall score of 2 stars out of a possible 5. However, chest compression measurements on the test dummy 'indicated an unacceptably high risk of serious or fatal injury. As a result, the final star in the adult occupant rating is struck-through'.

The first generation C5 is available as a five-door liftback or station wagon. Unlike its predecessors, the C5 is a liftback with a three-box design and a hatch. This form actually disguises the hatch, so Citroën has completely reversed the design philosophy from the fastback sedan era of Robert Opron. Power comes from by 1.8 and 2.0-litre straight-4 and 2.9-litre V6 petrol engines as well as 1.6, 2.0 and 2.2-litre direct injection diesel engines.

The C5 is the last Citroën developed under the chairmanship of Jacques Calvet (1982-1999), a period which saw the marque's historically distinctive design and engineering brand erode markedly.

The C5 had a further development of Citroën's hydropneumatic suspension, now called Hydractive 3. The major change with this system was the use of electronic sensors to replace the mechanical height correctors seen in all previous hydropneumatic cars. This allowed the suspension computer to automatically control ride height: at high speed the suspension is lowered to reduce drag and at low speeds on bumpy roads the ride height is raised. Manual control of ride height was retained, though it was overridden by the computer if the car was driven at an inappropriate speed for the selected height. Certain cars also featured the computer controlled ride stiffness seen on the Xantia and XM.

In a major break with Citroën tradition, the brakes and steering were no longer powered by the same hydraulic system as the suspension. It has been speculated that the primary driver for this was the cost of developing electronic brake force distribution for the system when the PSA Group already had an implementation for conventional brakes. Another factor may be the highly responsive nature of Citroën C5 brakes, which some have found hard to adjust to on other hydropneumatic cars, though it is felt by some to be superior. It can be scary for a C5 driver used to the instant reactions of an older hydropneumatic car to drive another vehicle and find an inch of pedal travel before any significant braking is achieved.

In 2004, the C5 underwent a major facelift (new front and rear ends; same centre section) to bring it into line with the look of the new Citroën C4. The liftback was lengthened from 4618 mm (181.8 in) to 4745 mm (186.8 in) and the station wagon from 4755 mm (187.2 in) to 4840 mm (190.6 in). Also this new version got swivelling directional headlights.

The Hydractive suspension improves ride quality and keeps the car leveled and can enable the car to drive on three wheels if one tire is flat. The suspension is derived from the Hydropneumatic suspension used in the 1950's Citroën DS. Variations in height using the Hydractive suspension range up to 15mm in the front and 11mm in the back.

The turbo power originates form two fixed turbochargers of identical size. Each of these can supply half the air input required to give the engine more power. Fuel mileage is 8.1 litres/100km - this was received from city and highway driving.

The Dodge Caliber offers a continuously variable transmission (dubbed CVT2 by Dodge) sourced from Jatco (a Nissan subsidiary), the second DaimlerChrysler model to employ this technology after the Mercedes-Benz A-Class. It uses a four-cylinder 1.8–2.4 L GEMA gasoline engine.

The car also features an optional electronically-controlled all-wheel drive system with variable torque between speeds of 25 and 65 mph (105 km/h) for optimal handling.

The Caliber rides on a heavily modified GS platform, co-designed with Mitsubishi Motors. The modified GS platform is now called JS platform by DCX for mid-size cars and PM/MK for compact cars. It shares the platform with the Mitsubishi Lancer, but is most similar to the Jeep Compass and Jeep Patriot.

The Caliber is built at the Belvidere Assembly (Illinois) plant, where its predecessor was produced.

The Caliber is an important vehicle for Chrysler in its quest to expand globally. The Caliber was one of Dodge's first modern offerings in Europe. Dodge also introduced the Caliber as part of its launch lineup in Asian markets such as Japan and Singapore, as it established new distribution channels there. It will be introduced in China in 2008 as Dodge's second modern vehicle offering in that market. Dodge vehicles were last officially sold in China during the World War II era. The introduction of the Caliber has also marked the return of the Dodge brand to Australia, for the first time since the early 1970's.

The base SE model features front-wheel drive and a 1.8 L 148 hp (110 kW) GEMA I4 attached to a Magna Drivetrain T355 5-speed manual transmission. A 2.0 L 158 hp (118 kW) version of the engine paired with the CVT2 transmission is available as an option.

The standard configuration for the SE lacks air conditioning, and does not have power windows, door locks, or mirrors. The grille surround is body-colored, while that of all other models is chromed. There is no tachometer, and no assist handles. 15 inch steel wheels with wheel covers are standard. Some options are not available on the SE.

The SRT-4 model, introduced at the Chicago Auto Show in February 2006, is a replacement for the original Neon-based SRT-4 produced by Chrysler's Street and Racing Technology group. It is a hatchback set to compete with the likes of the Volkswagen GTI and the Mazdaspeed 3. It features a 2.4-liter DOHC 16V Turbocharged I4 with dual variable valve timing (DVVT). It produces 285 hp (213 kW) at 6,400 rpm, and 265 lb·ft (359 N·m) of torque at 5,600 rpm using the Mitsubishi TD04HL4S-20 turbo. The engine is mated to a Getrag six-speed manual transmission, and utilizes a front-wheel drive drivetrain. The Caliber SRT-4 utilizes a high-performance MacPherson strut front suspension, and a performance-tuned multilink rear suspension.

The Bravo and Brava Mark 1 were replacements for Fiat's successful but ageing Tipo model. The cars came with all new engines, the base model using a 1.4 L 12-valve engine producing 80 bhp. Three other petrol engines were available: the 103 bhp 1.6 L 16-valve; the 113 bhp 1.8 L 16-valve engine and the top of the range 2.0 L 20-valve R5 unit used in the HGT model, which produced 147 bhp and which could take the car to a maximum speed of 135 mph (217 km/h). Two turbodiesel engines were also available: both were 1.9 L four cylinder units, one producing 75 bhp and the other making 100 bhp. Bravo/Brava was voted European Car of the Year on its launch.

In 1996 the Bravo/Brava chassis spawned saloon and estate versions, badged Fiat Marea, which won praise for its large boot. Another car based on the Bravo/Brava underpinnings was launched in 1998: the curious looking Fiat Multipla, a six-seater mini MPV.

The first generation Bravo/Brava was discontinued in Europe in late 2001, and replaced by the all-new Fiat Stilo, which was ultimately a sales flop in most countries where it was sold.

The second generation Fiat Bravo was introduced to the press in January 2007 in Rome, and later at the Geneva Motor Show in 2007. The new Bravo will be produced in Fiat's Cassino plant in Piedimonte S. Germano. The car was designed by Fiat Style Centre. Austrian automotive company Magna Steyr engineered a large amount of the car's body and internal fittings. CAD engineering and computer simulations were used on a very large scale with this model and the design was finished to a very tight schedule.

Blue&Me is a new feature first introduced with the Fiat Grande Punto and is fitted as standard on the Bravo Dynamic and Sport. Developed with Microsoft this system offers Bluetooth hands-free use with a mobile phone. It is also capable of displaying SMS text on the dash screen and it has built-in voice activation. Another part of the system is the inclusion of a USB connector so that an MP3 player or USB flashcard can be plugged in, giving the car's entertainment system access to MP3 files stored on the unit.

In Australia, the Fiat Bravo will be sold as the Fiat Ritmo, as Mazda Australia owns rights to the "Bravo" name. The Bravo will also be built in Brazil from late 2009 or early 2010, and will be sold there and throughout South America.

The new Bravo will be powered by three different petrol and two diesel engines. 'T-Jet' is the name of the new range of turbocharged petrol engines. The 150 PS T-Jet version has a Sport button to give an "overboost" function. At the end of 2007 the new 1.6 L M-jet diesel engine was launched, and a more powerful 120 PS (118 hp/88 kW) version in spring 2008. The 105 PS version is avaialable with the so-called "Eco" pack which gives better fuel consumption and lower CO_2 emissions (119 g/km). This engine is also Euro 5 rated.

FORD *Kuga*

The Ford Kuga is an upcoming compact crossover SUV to be produced by Ford Europe. The car is based on the C1 platform that also underpins the Ford Focus and Ford C-MAX. Both front-wheel drive and four-wheel drive will be offered, while only a 2.0-litre TDCi diesel engine will be available at launch.

The Kuga will go on sale in the first half of 2008, and will be built at Ford's plant in Saarlouis, Germany. In the UK, emphasising the car's premium market aspirations, only high-end Zetec and Titanium specifications will be offered. It's priced similar to the other small SUVs in the market such as the Citroen C-Crosser and the Vauxhall/Opel Antara, and is set to go on sale in the UK with a starting price of around £20,500.

On July 20, 2007, a report indicated that Ford executives were considering the prospects of sales in North America. This idea was later scrapped after it was determined the car could not be sold both competitively priced and at a profit in the US due to the current dollar-Euro exchange rate.

The fourth generation Mondeo (codename: CD345) was officially unveiled in 5-door production form in late 2006. Based on the EUCD platform developed with Volvo, the platform is the same used in the new large MPVs Galaxy and S-MAX, but not the North American Ford Fusion or the Mazda6 in Japan. It will also be used for several Volvos, for the new Land Rover Freelander, and even for the new Jaguar X-Type, though the latter may not be replaced.

The MK IV Ford Mondeo was released in May 2007 in the UK where it is currently available in five different trim levels: including Edge, Zetec, Ghia, Titanium and Titanium X. In February 2008, Ford announced that in some European markets the Mondeo will be made available with a new Titanium S series trim. This model aims to add an even more 'sporty character' than the current Titanium series. In March 2008, a new 2.2 175PS TDCi common-rail diesel engine will be available on Mondeo providing excellent power accelerating 0-60 mph in 8.4 seconds on the saloon and great fuel performance returning 45.6 mpg combined. Also available in March 2008 will be Mondeo ECOnetic based on the Zetec series. The Mondeo ECOnetic powered with a 1.8 125PS TDCI diesel will return CO_2 ratings of just 139 g/km on the 5 door.

Although the fourth production model, after the Mk III Galaxy, S-MAX and C-MAX, to adopt Ford's current 'kinetic' design language, the Mondeo's design theme was first seen on the Iosis concept shown at the 2005 Frankfurt Motor Show which gave an indication to the look of the Mk IV Mondeo. The new car, in estate bodystyle, was pre-launched in 'concept' form at the Paris Motor Show on 30 September 2006.

The new platform will allow for the use of Volvo's five-cylinder petrol engine, already featured in the Focus ST and S-Max. The petrol engines include a 1.6-litre with two power outputs (110PS & 125PS), the 2.0-litre (145 PS), 2.3-litre (161PS) for automatic models only and a 2.5-litre five cylinder turbo with 220 PS. Performance models may come with engines from Jaguar and Volvo

The new Mondeo will use the new electro-hydraulic steering system, first used on the C-MAX, that sharpens the steering response and helps to save fuel

A product placement promotional initiative made the Mk IV Mondeo James Bond's car for one incidental scene in Casino Royale, introducing the new model to global audiences in November 2006 on the launch day of the movie. Ford Group models have been prominent in the Bond franchise since 2002's Die Another Day, which featured an Aston Martin, a Jaguar convertible, and a Ford Thunderbird.

As with the previous model, the Mk IV Mondeo is not marketed in the US or Canada because Ford currently sells the same-class Fusion which was launched in 2005.

The Accord was originally planned to be a V6-powered car with a long hood and sporty pretensions. Honda chose the name Accord, reflecting "Honda's desire for accord and harmony between people, society and the automobile." The initial design was changed to a fuel efficient, low emission vehicle since it was introduced during the fuel crises of the 1970s. In the U.S. and Japan, a version was produced using Honda's CVCC technology, meeting emission standards of the 1970s and early 1980s without a catalytic converter.

Like the smaller Honda Civic, the Accord used front-wheel drive and a transverse engine layout. The Accord became the first Japanese car to be produced in the US in 1982, when production commenced in Marysville, Ohio at Marysville Auto Plant. It is also produced in Guangzhou, China by the Guangzhou Honda joint venture since 1999.

The Eighth generation Honda Accord does not offer a hybrid version, as Honda felt their "hybrid system works better on smaller cars". Instead, Honda offers a diesel version action of the Accord starting in the 2009 model year, which offers better fuel economy than the gasoline versions, and is 50-state emissions compliant. The Accord diesel for the US market was confirmed at the 2007 Tokyo Motor Show, and has been unveiled at the 2008 North American International Auto Show in Detroit, Michigan.

Honda has stated that the V6 models of the Accord features better fuel efficiency due to Honda's Variable Cylinder Management (VCM) system, which shuts off 2 or 3 of the cylinders depending on the type of driving (i.e. city driving, uphill/downhill driving, highway driving). This is supposed to increase the efficiency of the V6 models while keeping the power at 268 hp (200 kW). According to the Honda press release, the Accord Coupe V6 with the 6-speed manual transmission does not feature VCM. The lack of VCM results in a decrease of 4 MPG in highway fuel economy. In addition to VCM, the new V6 model of the Accord features more advanced emissions control technology, and complies with the California "Partial Zero-Emissions Vehicle" (PZEV) category. PZEV models of the Accord are automatic only. The 2008 model year also drops the 6-speed manual transmission from the sedan version.

The Accord received several key safety updates for the 2008 model year, most notably standard vehicle stability assist (VSA) and active front head restraints for all models. These new safety features contributed to perfect crash test scores for the Accord, earning it a "Top Safety Pick" designation from the Insurance Institute for Highway Safety (IIHS), an honor not bestowed upon most of the Accord's competitors.

The Jaguar X-TYPE is an compact executive car produced by the Ford owned British luxury marque Jaguar Cars since 2001. It is built on a modified version of the Ford CD132 platform, a British version of the Ford CDW27 platform, which is the base for the Ford Mondeo, and remains in production at Jaguar's Halewood facility in England.

The X-TYPE is the smallest of the current Jaguar saloon (sedan) cars, and was designed to build on the success of the S-Type, although it takes many styling cues from the XJ series. Jaguar states that 10% of the parts are made by Jaguar, 20% are made by Ford, while the rest are made by subcontractors.

The X-TYPE was designed as a direct competitor to the BMW 3 Series, Mercedes-Benz C-Class and the similar styled Rover 75. Sales have been poor (more noticeably in foreign markets than in the UK), however, blamed on its resemblance to the larger XJ which was traditionally bought by older customers, not the younger ones that Jaguar craved. Initially projected to surpass 100,000 annual sales, the X-TYPE peaked at 50,000 in 2003.

Sales in the United States, its primary market, dropped from 21,542 in 2004 to 10,941 in 2005. BMW sold 106,950 3 Series cars in the U.S. in 2005, while Mercedes-Benz sold 60,658 C-Class cars and Audi sold 48,922 A4 and S4 models. Despite these poor numbers, the X-TYPE is Jaguar's best-selling model, accounting for 36% of overall sales. Due to poor sales and the loss of profits resulting from the continued devaluation of the USD vs. the GBP in recent years, Ford (owner of the Jaguar brand) announced in October 2007, that it is stopping sales of the X-Type in the United States. Stock is expected to last through the first quarter of 2008. However, the new generation X-TYPE will go on sale in the UK in March 2008 and in other European markets in April 2008. In Canada, where it is Jaguar's best-selling vehicle, expect it to be sold there. As of March 2008, Jaguar has taken the X-type off of its North American site.

The X-TYPE is equipped with either a 192 hp (143 kW) 2.5 L or a 227 hp (169 kW) 3.0 L Jaguar AJ-V6 engine. All wheel drive (the patented Jaguar Traction 4 system) is standard on 2.5 L & 3.0 L variants, but the 2.0 L petrol and all diesel models are two wheel drive. There is no diesel version available in the U.S.

The four-wheel drive system is tuned to send 60% of engine power to the rear wheels and 40% to the front for a sportier feel. As of 2007 in the UK, the 2.0 L and 2.5 L V6 petrol variants have been discontinued. The 3.0 L is still available but only in estate form. The only saloon X-Types are the 2.0 L and 2.2 L Diesels.

The initial version of the X-TYPE was a saloon. In early 2004, this was joined by an estate version, making it the second ever Jaguar estate car, in addition to being the first to use a diesel engine. The estate version was launched to mixed reception. In the United States, the estate is officially known as the "Sportwagon" and is not available as a diesel.

The Mazda Atenza or Mazda 6 is a mid-size car produced by the Japanese car manufacturer Mazda since 2002. The name Atenza is used only in Japan with the Mazda 6 moniker used everywhere else in the world. The Atenza/Mazda 6 replaced the Capella/626, and has sold over one million units worldwide since its introduction, meaning it reached the one million mark faster than any previous Mazda.

The Mazda Atenza was the first of the new generation of 'Stylish', 'Insightful', and 'Spirited' range from Mazda. It was followed by the Mazda 2 in December 2002, RX-8 in August 2003, Mazda3 in January 2004, MX-5 in October 2005, and Mazda CX-7 in November 2006.

The Mazda Atenza is currently raced in the SCCA Pro Racing Speed World Challenge Touring Car Series. Mazda finished first in the manufacturer's championship standings. Mazda Atenza/6 drivers also finished first and second in the Touring Car driver points.

The Mazda6 second generation made its premiere at the Frankfurt auto show in September 2007. The US version will be redesigned for the 2009 model year, which will be a bigger car than the ones in other countries. Mazda followed Honda's strategy in offering a larger sedan in America compared to the European version, and the company believes the new car will strengthen the brand significantly. Engine choices include a new 2.5 liter 4-cylinder and North American versions get a 3.7 liter V6 sourced from the CX-9.

The new Atenza continues to provide 3 bodies, including 4-door saloon, 5-door hatchback and wagon. Despite its increase in dimensions, weight is not increased significantly and dynamics and fun of driving it could still retain. A number of journalists even praised its electrically assisted steering wheels for being considerably improved compared to the last generation, providing more feedback to the driver. The hatchback model even has a boot space with rear seats down beating the larger rival Ford Mondeo (hatchback) by 200 liters. For the American market though, only a sedan model will be available.

MERCEDES *C Class*

The Mercedes-Benz C-Class is a compact executive car produced by the Mercedes Car Group division of Daimler AG. First introduced in 1993 as a replacement for the 190 range, the C-Class was the most affordable model in the marque's lineup, until the 1997 arrival of the A-Class. The C-Class is built at Mercedes-Benz factories in Sindelfingen and Bremen, Germany, as well as in DaimlerChrysler's South African factory in East London. The very first W202 C-Class sedan was produced on June 1, 1993, and the second generation W203 C-Class rolled off the assembly line on July 18, 2000. The third generation W204 C-Class was launched in 2007.

DaimlerChrysler introduced a new generation of the C-Class on January 18, 2007 and displayed it in the 2007 Geneva Auto Show. Sales started on March 31, 2007 in almost all European countries. The new vehicle has an extended wheelbase and tracks, a stiffer bodyshell and a design inspired by the most recent S-Class and some hints from the CLS-Class. The model has three levels of equipment - Classic, Elegance and Avantgarde. A high performance AMG version with a 6.2 L engine followed in September 2007, labelled C 63 AMG with 457 PS (335 kW)to rival the Audi RS4 and BMW M3. The Classic and Elegance lines retain the traditional Mercedes-Benz radiator grille, with a three-point star bonnet emblem. The Avantgarde line has a grille similar to that on Mercedes' sport coupe models, with two horizontal bars and a large centre-mounted star. In the UK the Classic line is known as the SE and the Avantgarde line is known as the C-Class Sport , and comes with an AMG bodykit, and AMG alloy wheels as standard. The North American version is slightly different, as the Classic model is dropped. The Elegance is known as the C-Class Luxury and the Avantgarde wearing the AMG sports package is known as the C-Class sport. Both lines have an additional amber light in front of the front wheel well. New saloon and estate versions were announced in 2007, while the CLC-Class Sportcoupé will remain based on the W203 chassis. There will be an increase of component-sharing with other Mercedes' models, namely the redesigned E- and S-Class, as well as the upcoming GLK-Class compact SUV. One of the most technological breakthroughs of this car is a special system exclusive to this class, named 'Agility control' package. This is an innovative system, which through its unique concept provides drivers with excellent agility and the traditional, luxurious Mercedes ride quality. It achieves this feat through a complex hydro-mechanical set up, which constantly analyses road conditions and driving 'habits', resultantly it adjusts damper & suspension settings accordingly to provide the driver the best possible balance between ride comfort and agility. To take things still further , there is even an 'Advanced agility control' package drivers can opt for, this system is an upgrade to the standard one, offering a 'sport' mode button. The 'Advanced agility' package is a first for the C-class, and will be seen in future models, as the GLK.

NISSAN *Note*

The Nissan Note is a mini MPV produced by the Japanese manufacturer Nissan. The Japanese version has been on sale since 2004, and the European adaptation has gone on sale during 2006, with the United Kingdom first to launch, on 1st March. The car shares some of its underpinnings with the Renault Modus, and is designed to compete with the Opel/Vauxhall Meriva and Fiat Idea as well as the Renault offering. It is manufactured at Nissan's plant in Sunderland, England.

The car is positioned as a roomy car and includes special add-ons for family needs. The key feature is the flexibility of the interiors. Even a person as tall as 2.00 metres (6.6 ft) can fit in either the driver's seat or the back seat easily. It is designed to be a cross segment car. Another design detail of this car is the boomerang-shaped rear light. Nissan aims to appeal to the family car shoppers with this car by including children-friendly features.

The Nissan Note used to be available in three specifications, the 'S', 'SE' and 'SVE'. The base model came in with full electric windows, alloy wheels and front fog lights or the Flexi-Board boot system. The SE saw the introduction of 16" Alloys, Air Con, front fog lights and Flexi-Board Boot and the SVE had Climate Control, Rear Privacy Glass, 17" Alloys and ESP. These models have been replaced with the Visia, Acenta, Acenta R and the Tekna. The Visia is almost identical to the old 'S' model whereas the Acenta, Acenta R and Tekna now come complete with MP3 Auxiliary jack and Bluetooth Car Stereo as no cost options.

The Peugeot 308 is a small family car produced by the French car manufacturer PSA. It was unveiled on June 5, 2007 and is the first car of the 008 generation of Peugeot models.

Loosely intended as the replacement for the Peugeot 307 (which remains in production), the new vehicle was based upon the old 307's chassis, while having a different bodywork and being slightly larger in size.

The Peugeot 308 currently holds the record of the most fuel efficient mainstream car, averaging 3.13 L/100 km (75 mpg–U.S. / 90 mpg–imp) over a distance of 14,580 kilometres (9,060 mi).

In the United Kingdom (a major market for Peugeot, and where some of their models are made), television adverts aired with the slogan "the drive of your life". The development code for the car was "Project T7".

The pictures set for official unveiling were leaked on May 31, 2007, a week ahead of schedule. Sales began in September 2007.

A 2+2 coupé concept car development of the 308, the Peugeot 308 RC Z, was presented by Peugeot at the 2007 Frankfurt Motor Show. This coupé concept is 18 cm lower than the standard car. It has similar proportions to the Audi TT.

A station wagon concept version of the 308, the Peugeot 308 SW Prologue, was also unveiled at the 2007 Frankfurt Motor Show. In February 2008 the production version was announced, to go on sale in the UK in June that year. The finished product went on show at the 78th International Geneva Motor Show in March 2008.

A cabriolet with a retractable hardtop is also expected to eventually arrive and replace the Peugeot 307 CC. Cost is predicted to be around £20,000, to compare with other small executive coupés.

In the UK, the basic 308 1.4 litre 3-door hatchback is expected to retail at around £12,000 — a similar price to the equivalent 307 that it replaces. It is cheaper than the Honda Civic, similarly priced to the Volkswagen Golf, but slightly more expensive than the Ford Focus and Vauxhall Astra.

Robert Bosch GmbH is supplying hybrid diesel-electric technology to Peugeot 308. A prototype 308 equipped with this technology was displayed in the Frankfurt car show '07.

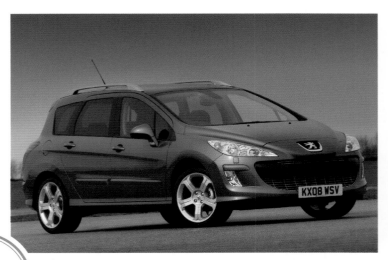

"Eurovans" is a common name applied to nearly identical large MPVs resulting from Sevel, a joint-venture of PSA and Fiat, and manufactured at Sevel Nord factory in France, near Valenciennes. The first eurovans were sold as Citroën Evasion (Synergie), Fiat Ulysse, Lancia Zeta and Peugeot 806. The present, second generation, saw the renaming of all but the Ulysse to Citroën C8, Lancia Phedra and Peugeot 807 respectively.

The eurovans differ little technically and visually, being a prime example of badge engineering. The eurovans share mechanicals and body structure with Sevel light commercial vans, Citroën Jumpy (Dispatch), Fiat Scudo and Peugeot Expert. They are more technically related to PSA than Fiat vehicles, as PSA governs the Sevel Nord part of the joint-venture.

The first-generation eurovans were superseded by a new model in 2002. The floorpan, wheelbase and suspension setup were not altered, but all exterior dimensions as well as front and rear tracks were increased. In particular, the increase in length by almost 30 cm greatly enhanced interior capacity. The new eurovans were afforded a much more bubbly, contemporary look, along with a modern-looking dashboard with centrally mounted gauges. The differences are now more pronounced, encompassing entire front fascias and rear sections (including head- and taillights), as well as different interior color themes. The Fiat and the Lancia are slightly wider than PSA vans, and the Phedra is also longer than other eurovans .

Except for the Fiat Ulysse, all the models have been renamed. The 806 was, as expected, replaced by 807, while Citroën chose to put the minivan in line with its new naming theme, where models were called Cx (x being a number roughly corresponding to the relative size of a given model), hence the Citroën C8. As the new Lancias didn't use Greek letters anymore, the new minivan was called Lancia Phedra, in honor of the Greek mythological figure Phaedra.

To highlight the launch of the V6 engine, Peugeot presented a design study called Peugeot 807 Grand Toursime at the 2003 Geneva Motor Show. Apart from the exquisite appointment of the 4-passenger interior and some mechanical and visual tuning, the car was essentially a top-of-the-line 807 in a peculiar purple color.

At the end of 2000, after almost seven years of production, the original Laguna was replaced by an all-new model which shared its chassis with the Nissan Primera (which arrived a year later). The engines were upgraded and the equipment list made longer. Widely regarded as one of the safest vehicles on the road today, it was the first vehicle available in Europe to achieve 5 stars in the EuroNCAP crash test results, a feat which was soon followed by all other models in Renault UK's current model line-up. The Laguna featured a 'keyless' ignition system which, instead of a key, used a credit card style device to unlock the car and start the engine - although the card is expensive to replace. The styling of the second generation Laguna was heavily influenced by the Initiale concept car.

The Laguna estate was only available with five seats, unlike the previous model which has seven seats as an option on some versions. It was badged SportsTourer or Grandtour depending on the country, and was marketed as a lifestyle vehicle rather than a load carrier.

The Laguna II had relaunch in March 2005, according to Renault with improved security, driving performance and comfort. It also had a moderate redesign of the air intake at the front of the car, now matching the design of the Megane. A electronic handbrake was also introduced, this was previously seen on the Scenic and Espace The engines were much the same as before, with the 1.6 and 1.8 petrol units being offered in some markets, while other countries get a 2.0 petrol unit (turbo or non-turbo) and two diesels (1.9 or 2.2 direct-injection). After facelift Laguna comes with the third and whole new diesel engine 2.0 dCi with 150 hp (112 kW) and 175 hp (130 kW),this one the most powerful 2 liter diesel engine in the world as of May 2007.

The Renault Laguna III was officially announced in a press release on June 4, 2007 . The car was unveiled to the public at the Frankfurt Motor Show in September, and it went on sale in October 2007. The car comes both as a 5-door liftback and as a 5-door estate. This third generation is based on the platform D, shared with the Nissan Altima and the Nissan Murano.

Laguna III is the first car to have gone through Aubevoye Technical Centre's Electro-Magnetic Compatibility unit in the course of its development.

The Toyota Auris is a compact 3 door and 5 door hatchback which shares the same E platform with the Toyota Corolla. In Europe, Toyota positioned the Auris as the replacement of Corolla Hatchback, while the notchback Sedan continued by the Corolla nameplate. The Auris succeeds the Corolla RunX in Japan and the RunX (no Corolla badging) in South Africa.

Toyota Australia and Toyota New Zealand resisted suggestions from Toyota Japan to adopt the new European Auris name for the Corolla citing the experience of Nissan Australia where the Tiida replaced the well known Pulsar name. The new Corolla was released in Australia in May-June, 2007. The Toyota Matrix redesign will be based on the Auris.

The Auris was released on February 1 2007 in the UK and the Turkey plant. It replaces the Toyota Corolla hatchback. With a fresh design and upmarket features including an MP3/WMA player. Toyota aims to position the Auris at the higher end of the lower-medium segment to lure buyers from competing cars such as Volkswagen Golf and the Alfa Romeo 147. Trim levels are T2, T3, and T Spirit. The higher end T180 model went on sale in the UK during April 2007.

The upscale sister of Auris is called Toyota Blade. It replaces the Toyota Allex, which, in turn, was the replacement for the Toyota Sprinter. It has different nose and tail, and is powered by Toyota's 2.4 liter 2AZ-FE engine. Recently Toyota released the Blade Master and Blade Master G, an upgraded trim of the Blade which features Toyota's 280 PS 3.5 L 2GR-FE V6 engine, larger brakes, and an upgraded suspension.

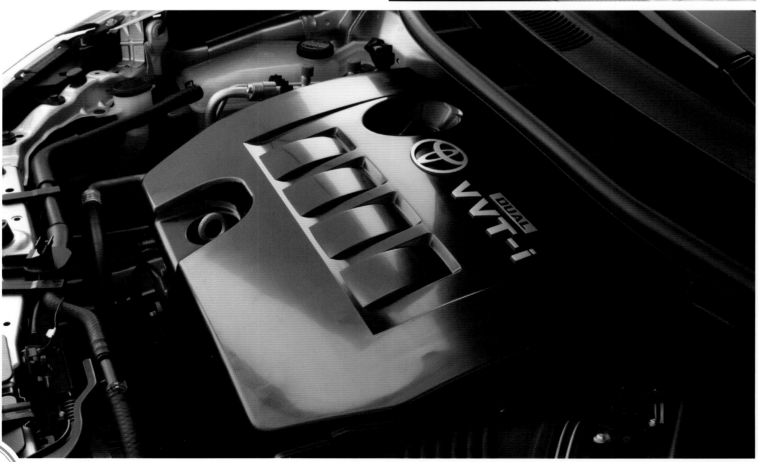

Astra is a model-name which has been used by Vauxhall, the British subsidiary of General Motors (GM), on their small family car ranges since 1979. Astras are technically essentially identical with similar vehicles offered by GM's German subsidiary Opel in most other European countries. For the first two generations, the nameplate was applied to UK spec right-hand drive versions of Opel Kadett (which it was sold as in the Republic of Ireland in right-hand drive), and since 1991, Opel also uses the Astra nameplate, so Vauxhall and Opel Astras are essentially identical vehicles. General Motors' Saturn division in America also offers the Astra since late 2007.

GM Europe launched Astra H/C in March 2004. Based on the then-new Delta platform, its size was increased compared to the previous version. Each engine is provided with its own Lotus-tuned suspension settings.

The Astra H/C was first launched as a five-door hatchback, which by the end of 2004 was joined by a five-door Caravan estate and a sporty three-door hatchback, designated the GTC for European markets, Sport Hatch in the UK and the Coupé in Australia. The GTC has the option of a windscreen called "panoramic windscreen" (unique for a production car at the time of its launch) which extends into the roof area.

Chevrolet do Brazil did not launch the Astra H/C production, keeping the previous model as Chevrolet Astra sold in many South American countries (yet the newer model is sold as Chevrolet Astra in Mexico and from 2006 in Chile), but it has developed a 4-door sedan based on the Astra H/C, which has been launched as the Chevrolet Vectra in 2005. The Chevrolet Vectra utilises a longer (2.70 m - 106.3 in) wheelbase, with its platform is borrowed from the Zafira minivan. It replaced the Vectra B, which was still available in Brazil until that date. On 19 October 2006 at the international auto show in Istanbul, Turkey, Opel launched this version of the sedan, to be manufactured in Gliwice as an Opel for several Eurasian markets. At that time, a 3-door van variant of the wagon was introduced by Vauxhall in Britain. In May 2007, GM Brazil announced the launch of the 5-door Astra H/C, as the Chevrolet Vectra GT, to differentiate from the already existing Astra G/B, which will remain in production.

During 2005 Opel introduced the OPC version of the Astra GTC (Astra VXR in the UK) which is powered by an updated version of the 2.0 L turbo ecotec engine producing 240 PS (177 kW) and 320 N·m (236 ft·lbf) of torque. Standard features of the OPC version include sports bodykit and interior, a six-speed manual gearbox, xenon headlamps and 18" alloys wheels amongst others.

The Opel Insignia is a mid-size car that will replace the Opel Vectra and will debut at the 2008 London Motor Show. It will be sold exclusively in Europe, but in the United Kingdom, it will be known as the Vauxhall Insignia. It will be around 200 mm (7.9 in) larger than the current Vectra, and will be built on the new GM Epsilon II platform. Addressing the faults of the current Vectra, Opel is aiming the new Insignia more upmarket by using better quality materials and improving its exterior styling.

Opel suggested the Insignia will draw styling inspiration from the GTC concept car it displayed earlier at the 2007 Geneva Motor Show. Opel first used the Insignia name on a radical concept unveiled at the Frankfurt Motor Show in 2003.

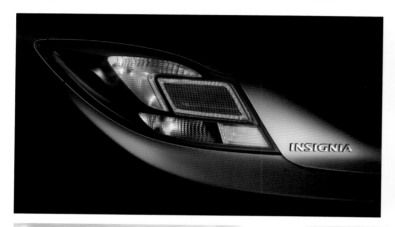

The original V70 was a development of the Volvo 850 station wagon and sedan series. The new name reflected Volvo's new strategy of naming vehicles depending on size and body style. Thus, the 850 was deemed to be a relative size 70. The name is then appended with the type of vehicle. So the station wagon adopted V (for Versatility), S (for Saloon) and C (for the new Coupé); these cars are respectively known as V70, S70 and C70. There were 1,800 improved and new parts in the design from the original 850, including upgraded passive and active safety, better handling and new engines. Gone were the 850's square edges and replaced by rounded corners to suit the late 90s style trend. Other changes included a new 'family face' for the V/S/C70 models, colour coded bumpers, clear indicator lenses, and a new dashboard fascia and materials. However on the whole, one could say the car was similar to its predecessor, but nevertheless, a successful facelift.

In the end of 1999 (2001 for North America), Volvo released the all-new V70 based on the new P2 platform which itself was first used for the entirely Swedish-designed Volvo S80 sedan in 1997. This new car dispensed with the boxy shape of Volvos before it to take on a curvy profile much like the S40/S60 series, and added a new aggressive front end. Where the first generation V70 had a saloon variant (S70), the second generation lost the S70 as the new S80 was now seen to be the 'S70 for the new millennium'. The second generation of the V70 will finish production for model year 2007.

The V70 shares the same sheet metal ahead of the B-pillar with the Volvo S60, although the grilles are different and the front bumpers are mildly different. The dashboard and the majority of the interior of both cars are the same.

As was the case with all P2 platform Volvos, a minor refresh of the V70 occurred across all markets for the 2005 model year, which brought minor styling changes to the front facia, tail lamps, along with several improvements and changes to the interior fittings.

Volvo continues to market the V70 second generation in Europe and Scandanavia, under the name V70 Classic.

The third V70 was officially unveiled by Volvo on 2 February 2007. The car was developed to be a slightly more up-market car than the previous model, but remains the same size. Despite this, rear-seat legroom is increased two centimetres and a revised tailgate design increases the load area volume by 55 L. The tailgate now has motorized lift and closing action. The interior is one of the most luxurious in its class.

As with the second-generation V70, the new car is a unique design sharing little externally with other Volvo models. The Volvo P24 platform is used and much of the interior (other than the rear seats and loadbay) are shared with the second generation S80. The new V70 will have a 3.2 L I6, a 3.0 L turbo straight-six, a light-pressure turbo 2.5 L I5, and two 2.4 L I5 diesel engines. Only the last two are offered with manual gearboxes.

The Audi Q7 is a full-size SUV produced by German automaker Audi since its unveiling at the Los Angeles Auto Show in January 2006.

In it's name Q7, the "Q" denotes a new family of vehicles for Audi, and the designation "7" marks its placement between the A6 and A8 in Audi's model range.

The Q7 utilizes a modified version of the Volkswagen 7L platform. Based on the Audi Pikes Peak quattro concept car, the Q7 is designed more for on-road use and was not meant for serious off-road use where a transfer case is needed, but in an offroad test through the Australian Out-Back it fared remarkably well for a luxury "soft roader". Although it lacks a low-range transfer case, it has a central differential lock and an adjustable-height air suspension which helps in offroad situations. Audi South Africa runs a very tough offroad course with the Q7 where it actually proves itself a better off-roader than most would give it credit for. In accordance to the charters it has been argued that the Audi had nothing at all to do with the Volkswagen.

Audi's 350 PS (345 hp/257 kW), 440 N·m (325 ft·lbf) 4163 cc V8 and 280 PS (276 hp/206 kW), 360 N·m (266 ft·lbf) V6 3596 cc petrol engines, both with FSI technology, are offered. Interestingly, Q7 using either engine has the same 0 - 100 km/h performance.

Two diesel options are available; a 240 PS (237 hp/177 kW) 3.0L V6 and in mid-2007 the 4.2 litre 331 PS (326 hp/243 kW) diesel with 760 N·m (561 ft·lbf) torque known from the Audi A8 was introduced. Audi is reportedly going to introduce a hybrid version of the Q7 in 2008

To underline the racing success of its diesel engined Le Mans-winning R10 racer, Audi presented a concept-version of the car with a new V12 TDI Q7 at the 2006 Paris Auto Show. It uses piezo fuel injectors like the 2007 Mercedes E320 CDI. The twin-turbodiesel six-litre engine generates 500 PS (493 hp/368 kW) and 1,000 N·m (738 ft·lbf) of torque, making it the most powerful diesel engine, and also the only twelve-cylinder diesel engine, used in any passenger car. The diesel can pull the Q7 from rest to 100 km/h in 5.5 seconds.

quattro GmbH is currently developing, and will subsequently produce the most powerful diesel powered SUV in its class. The Audi Q7 V12 TDI quattro will be fitted with a V12 TDI. A world first, this all new diesel engine displaces 6 Litres, generating 368 kW (500 hp), and a massive 1,000 Nm of torque. This is enough to complete the 0-100 k/ph dash in 5.5 seconds, making it perform like modern sports cars.

The BMW X6 is a mid-size luxury crossover SUV released for sale in the second quarter of 2008 by German automaker BMW. The X6 combines the attributes of an SUV (high ground clearance, all wheel drive and all-weather ability, large wheels and tires) with the stance of a coupé (bold styling, dramatic sloping roof).

It is built in BMW's North American plant in Spartanburg, South Carolina alongside the BMW X5 whose platform it shares. It is dubbed "Sports Activity Coupé" by BMW, and while slightly longer and wider than the X5 is significantly lower and seats only four people. The concept model debuted at the 2007 Frankfurt Auto Show. The production X6 officially debuted at the 2008 Detroit International Auto Show. A hybrid version, which will be the first such vehicle from BMW, was also announced. it is built by bmw and goes about 100 miles per hour.

Initially, the BMW X6 is available in North America in two variants. Both use twin-turbocharged engines. The top-of-the-line model is the xDrive50i which uses an all-new 4.4-liter twin-turbocharged V8 engine. It produces 407 horsepower (303 kW) between 5,500 and 6,400 rpm, and 600 N·m (443 ft·lbf) of torque over a wide range of between 1,800 and 4,500 rpm. It is the first production turbocharged V8 engine in the world to feature its turbochargers between the V section in the middle of the two banks of cylinders.

The other model is the X6 xDrive35i powered by the N54 3.0-liter twin-turbocharged inline-six gasoline engine, producing 306 horsepower (228 kW) between 5,800 and 6,250 rpm, and a peak torque of 400 N·m (295 ft·lbf) between 1,400 and 5,000 rpm. This engine also sees duty in the 1, 3 and 5 Series BMW cars.

Two diesel variants have been announced, and are expected to constitute as much as 90% of sales volume in European markets. The models are called the xDrive30d and xDrive 35d, respectively. They are powered by BMW's 3.0-liter turbodiesel engine (in its sequential twin-turbocharged variant for the xDrive35d), and output 235 hp (xDrive30d) and 286 hp (xDrive 35d). The second of these power units will form the basis of BMW's Diesel launch in 50 USA states late in 2008.

The X6 marks BMW's first use of its new Dynamic Performance Control system, which works in unison with xDrive all-wheel drive (both are standard on the X6). DPC is a drivetrain and chassis control system that works to regulate traction and especially correct over- and understeer by actively spreading out drive forces across the rear axle. Torque is split not only between the front and rear wheels (xDrive) but also from side to side at the rear for improved agility and added stability (through the DPC rear axle).

The Citroën C-Crosser is a compact crossover SUV, designed for the French manufacturer Citroën, and produced by Mitsubishi Motors on the basis of the new Outlander. The equivalent Peugeot badge-engineered version will be the 4007. It was expected that the car would be named the C7, but it has been announced that it will now be called the C-Crosser. The C-Crosser has taken its name from the four-wheel drive concept car that Citroën first displayed in the 2001 Frankfurt Motor Show.

Occupants will benefit from the easily reconfigured second and third row of seats, which can be folded away quickly and effortlessly to provide a flat floor and vast load space. The rear two seats can be completely hidden away under the floor, while the second row of seating, slides to offer greater leg room or boot space, features a 60:40 split/fold function that is operated via electric controls in the boot. This allows for the car to be used for both sporting and also for transporting groups of up to 7 people, including the driver. This is similar to the seating arrangement in the new Citroën C4 Picasso which also offers the capability of seating 7 persons.

The C-Crosser's integral transmission allows drivers to have a choice of three settings, dependent on road conditions and driving style: two-wheel drive, four-wheel drive and a lock setting designed for low-grip conditions. Ensuring an optimum blend of comfort, road holding and off-road capability. All these transmissions are selectable using the control behind the gear lever.

DODGE *Nitro*

The Dodge Nitro is a compact SUV from the Dodge division of Chrysler LLC. Launched for the 2007 model year at the Chicago Auto Show, the Nitro shares its platform with the Jeep Liberty. It is assembled at the Toledo North Assembly Plant in Toledo, Ohio. This Jeep facility is part of a complex including the Toledo South Assembly Plant, home to the Jeep Wrangler since the 1940s. The Nitro went into production in August 2006 and went on sale in September. The Nitro is also Dodge's first compact SUV since the Raider was discontinued in 1990.

The Nitro is priced at US$19,885. It is one of the first modern Dodge-branded cars on sale in Europe since its introduction in early 2007. All Nitros are available with rear-wheel drive, part-time all-wheel drive is available as an option. The top-line Nitro R/T with all-wheel drive sells for $27,630 . It was Dodge's entry-level SUV until the 2009 model year, when the larger, car-based Dodge Journey crossover SUV arrived to be priced below the Nitro.

Dodge is touting the car's "Load 'N Go" sliding cargo floor as a major selling feature. Similar to a system offered on the Saab 9-5 station wagon, the floor can be extended through the rear hatch by 18 in (457 mm) to ease loading.

Another purported attribute of the car is its SUV/hot rod styling blend, complete with unmistakably pronounced fenders.

A van version, with the second row of seats removed and the cargo area windows blacked out, is available in select European markets.

FORD *Explorer*

The Explorer and Mountaineer were updated for 2006 on a new frame, produced by Magna International rather than Tower Automotive. It was upsized, because the Ford Freestyle (now called Ford Taurus X), slotted between it and the Escape. Along with this new, stronger base were a new interior, redesigned rear suspension, and power-folding third-row seats. A tire-pressure monitoring system and electronic stability control are standard. Power running boards (like those on the Lincoln Navigator) that lower to allow easier to access for someone entering the vehicle and then later retract upon door closure are available. Unlike previous Explorers, there will be no right-hand drive version. Ford Australia has a capable local equivalent instead, being the Australian designed and developed Ford Territory. The new Explorer is marketed in Japan in a left-hand drive configuration, as LHD vehicles are considered prestigious there.

A 210 hp (157 kW) 4.0 L V6 is the base engine, with the 292 hp (218 kW) 24-valve V8, similar to the Mustang engine, as the top choice. A six-speed automatic transmission is available with this engine as well. The Explorer was nominated for the North American Truck of the Year award for 2006.

A new Sport Trac was added to the Explorer line in early 2006 for the 2007 model year. Unlike its predecessor it sold through 2005, it will feature the V8 engine as an option, and will be based on the new, larger Explorer platform. AdvanceTrac with Roll Stability Control will be standard in the Sport Trac.

HONDA *CR-V*

A redesigned CR-V was launched for the 2007 model year. The third generation CR-V is powered by the latest version of Honda's standard K-series 2.4 L 4-cylinder engine, similar variants of which can also be found in the current-generation Honda Accord and Honda Element. A 2.4 L engine upgraded to 166 hp is used in the North American market. A 2.2 L i-CTDI diesel is offered in the European and Asian markets. The European market Honda CR-V offers a new R20A 2.0 L engine, based on the Honda R-series i-VTEC SOHC engine found in the Honda Civic, as opposed to the previous CR-V offering the K20A. The manual transmission has been dropped from the US market, leaving the five speed automatic as the sole unit.

The 2007 CR-V features a rear liftgate, unlike previous models. There is no longer a spare wheel attached to the back door. The new CR-V is lower, wider and shorter than the previous models; the length decrease stems mostly from the fact that the spare wheel no longer adds length to the back of the vehicle. A lowering of the center of gravity is another benefit of the spare wheel being located underneath the rear floor. A feature unique amongst SUVs is the center rear seat pass-through.

Honda is also offering an integrated Navigation option on the EX-L model. The navigation unit is made for Honda by Alpine and includes voice activated control, XM radio, in dash CD player that can play MP3's and WMA's. It also has a 6 Disc CD changer in the center console and a PC Card (PCMCIA) slot in the Nav unit for flash memory MP3 or WMA files. A second CD player is behind the navigation screen, this CD player plays MP3/WMA cds. A rear backup camera is also included.

An iPod adapter was to be an available option on US models, but is currently only available as an add-on accessory. Even so, all CR-V models still have the auxiliary audio input jack, which is either on the head unit itself (LX) or on central tray (EX) or inside the center console (all versions of the EX-L, with or without navigation).

In the United States, the Honda CR-V became the number-one selling SUV in the US for 2007, a title previously held for fifteen years (1991–2006) by the Ford Explorer. To meet the extremely high demand, Honda shifted some Civic production from East Liberty, Ohio to Alliston Plant #2 (where some Pilot, Ridgeline, and Odyssey production was located until production was consolidated at Honda's Lincoln, Alabama facility) to free up space for additional CR-V production. Currently, the East Liberty plant is building 180+ CR-Vs a day for the US and Canadian markets, and additional vehicles for both markets are also being imported from Japan and Mexico. Notably, the Mexican-built CR-Vs are assembled from CKD (complete knock-down) kits made in East Liberty.

The Honda Pilot is Honda's second SUV fully built and designed by Honda, released in the summer of 2002 for the 2003 model year. The Honda Pilot is built in Lincoln, Alabama and was built in Alliston, Ontario, Canada up until April 2007. The Pilot is now built exclusively at the Lincoln, Alabama plant. Honda's initial SUV offering for many years was the Passport, which was a rebadged Isuzu Rodeo. Where the Passport was truck-based, it replaced the extended-wheelbase EX trim of the Passport. The Pilot shares underpinnings and the powertrain with the Acura MDX, which has a lineage which can be traced to the Honda Odyssey minivan. The Pilot's unibody construction, however, is fortified with integrated perimeter frame rails, which helps it withstand light off-road use.

The Pilot was designed to fill a large American demand for SUVs. Prior to the introduction of the Pilot, Honda only had the smaller CR-V based on the Civic, and the aforementioned Passport. However, the CR-V lacked in features many American consumers looked for in an SUV, which are overall size, passenger space, and towing capacity. The Pilot is at most designed to withstand light-duty off-roading. The Pilot has been a best-seller for Honda, with Honda selling over 100,000 Pilots in 2004, an increase of almost 20% over 2003. The Pilot is sold in North America, while Japan and Australia get its relative, the Honda MDX instead. In the Middle East, the Pilot is sold as the Honda MR-V.

For 2006, the Pilot received new front and rear fascias, a redesigned interior, and various standard safety features. The Pilot is capable of transporting up to eight passengers. The third row seats 3 but legroom is limited, allowing transportation of small children or adults on short trips. Similar to the Honda Odyssey, the rear seats are capable of folding into completely flat surfaces to allow larger cargo inside if necessary. Seats are configured as stadium seating. Optional amenities that can also be included are a powered moonroof, DVD entertainment system, and a navigation system.

The Pilot employs a four-wheel drive system called Variable Torque Management 4WD (VTM-4). The VTM-4 system delivers power to all four wheels under acceleration and when wheel slippage is detected. The VTM-4 system has a dashboard switch that locks both rear half-shafts to get the driver unstuck, but it operates in just the first two gears and unlocks at 18 mph (29 km/h). Otherwise, the system operates primarily in front-wheel drive and sends torque to the rear wheels when spin is detected up front. Two wheel drive models have been available since 2006.

The Pilot's safety mechanisms are the VTM-4 system, ABS-equipped four-wheel disc brakes, rack-and-pinion steering, four-wheel independent suspension and 282° of outward visibility. The foundation for the Pilot is a highly rigid unibody with reinforcing structures and energy absorbing crush zones. The Pilot's structure is designed to deform progressively in front, side and rear end collisions.

JEEP *Grand Cherokee*

The Grand Cherokee's origins date back to 1983 when American Motors (AMC) engineers were designing a successor to the smaller Jeep Cherokee (XJ). Three designers — Larry Shinoda, Adam Clenet, and Giorgetto Giugiaro — were under contract with AMC to create and build a clay model of the replacement model, then known as the "XJC" project. However, the basic design for the Cherokee's replacement was well under way by AMC's in-house designers and the 1989 Jeep Concept 1 show car foretold the basic design.

The Grand Cherokee was the first Chrysler-badged Jeep product. Development work for the new model continued and Chrysler employees (after the 1987 buyout of AMC) were eager for a late-1980s release date; however, then-CEO Lee Iacocca was pushing for redesigned Chrysler minivans, thus delaying the Grand Cherokee's release until late 1992 as an Explorer competitor.

The Grand Cherokee debuted in grand fashion at the 1992 North American International Auto Show in Detroit, Michigan. Then-Chrysler president Robert Lutz drove Detroit mayor, Coleman Young up the steps of Cobo Hall and through a plate glass window to show off the new vehicle. Production of the Grand Cherokee started shortly afterward in the purpose-built Jefferson North Assembly in Detroit, Michigan and has remained there since.

The all-new WK Grand Cherokee debuted in 2004 for the 2005 model year. Features available for the first time in a Jeep included Quadra-Drive II four-wheel drive, rear-seat DVD player and optional 5.7L Hemi V-8.

The design still emphasizes power and luxury, with significant work done on improving noise, vibration, and harshness (NVH). However, for the first time, Jeep also emphasized on-road performance to a similar extent as the cornerstone of its brand, off-road capability.

This newfound emphasis on on-road refinement led Jeep to replace the live-axle with leading-arms front suspension (found in the ZJ and WJ) with a new design: an independent double-wishbone setup like that which debuted in the 2002 Liberty. The new Jeep changed its philosophy due to what it perceived as increasing demand in the SUV marketplace for on-road performance and decreasing demand for off-road capability, and though the new design is perceived to be more smooth over washboard-types of roads, the new front suspension was criticized by off-roading Jeep community for its inability to provide optimal axle articulation during low-speed, technical maneuvers, specifically over uneven terrain.

JEEP *Patriot*

The Jeep Patriot (MK) is a compact SUV introduced in early 2007 for the 2007 model year by the Jeep marque of DaimlerChrysler. It debuted publicly in April 2006 at the New York Auto Show. It slots between the Liberty and Compass in the Jeep lineup with pricing starting from US$14,985, making it the least-expensive sport utility vehicle in North America.

The Patriot and Compass are both based on the DaimlerChrysler/Mitsubishi GS platform. These vehicles are differentiated by their styling and marketing: The Patriot is a traditional four-door Jeep wagon, similar to the Cherokee, which was discontinued in the U.S. in 2001, while the Jeep Compass is intended as a sporty crossover, but with more capacity to handle rough roads and poor weather than competitors like the Pontiac Vibe. The Dodge Caliber, also based on the GS platform, is a more direct competitor to the Pontiac Vibe and Toyota Matrix, and is more like a small hatchback wagon than either of the Jeeps. The Patriot is manufactured at DaimlerChrysler's Belvidere, Illinois assembly plant alongside the Dodge Caliber and Compass.

The Patriot uses a four-cylinder 2.4 L GEMA gasoline I4 engine and also has a 2.0 L Volkswagen-designed diesel engine for the European and Australian markets. The base car features front-wheel drive, but a choice of two electronically-controlled four-wheel drive systems is optional. One, the Freedom Drive I, is a full-time system for on-road use. Freedom Drive II is made for off-road use with variable torque between speeds of 25 and 65 mph for optimal handling. The 2.0 L GEMA I4 is an option for the 4X2 model Patriot.

The Freedom Drive II-equipped Patriot uses a continuously variable transmission with a low range instead of a traditional two-speed transfer case, but has Jeep's "Trail Rated" badging, signifying that it "has been designed to perform in five categories of off-road conditions: traction, ground clearance, maneuverability, articulation, and water fording." The Freedom Drive II Patriot is among the most offroad-capable vehicles in its class.

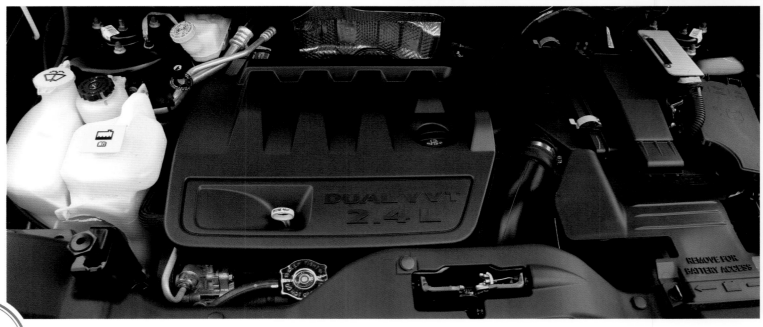

LAND ROVER *Discovery*

The Discovery is a four wheel drive on-road and off-road vehicle from the British car maker Land Rover. There have been three generations of the vehicle, which is less expensive than the company's top Range Rover model. The Discovery was introduced in the late 1980s and is the most popular model from Land Rover. It is less utilitarian than the Defender, but it is very competent off road. The current Discovery Series III is marketed in North America as the LR3.

On 2 April 2004, owners Ford Motor Company introduced a new Discovery 3 (or LR3 in North America) for the 2005 model year. The Series II Discovery was long over-due for replacement. Although still a capable and popular vehicle, its chassis, coil-spring suspension and beam-axle layout had changed very little since the launch of the original Discovery in 1989. In turn, that vehicle used essentially the same underpinnings as the original Range Rover, launched in 1970. The Discovery II was beginning to lose sales to more sophisticated 'working' 4x4 vehicles from Japan (such as the Toyota Land Cruiser and Mitsubishi Shogun) and 'sports' 4x4s from Europe (such as the BMW X5 and Mercedes-Benz M-Class). A replacement vehicle had been planned for many years, but the project had been delayed many times due to the break up of the Rover Group in 2000 and the need to replace the Range Rover in 2001.

The Discovery 3 was an entirely new design, sharing not a single component with the outgoing model. Its styling is still traditional Land Rover, with function dictating the look, rather than fashion, and with lots of horizontal and vertical lines. It retains the key features of the Discovery, such as the stepped roofline and steeply-raked windscreen. The LR3 name was chosen for North American markets due to negative quality associations with the Discovery name and (according to Land Rover) a preference in the American market for alpha-numeric model designations (the Freelander 2 would also be re-designated for the North American market- in this case as the LR2).

Construction-wise, Land Rover developed an all-new method which they called Integrated Body Frame (IBF). The previous Discovery models had used a traditional, strong ladder-frame chassis. Whilst tough in off-road use, these are heavy and detract from the on-road handling of the vehicle. Monocoque vehicles are more rigid, giving improved high-speed handling, but can be damaged by the stresses involved in heavy off-road use. In the IBF the body, engine bay and passenger compartment is built as a monocoque, which is mated to a basic ladder-chassis holding the gearbox and suspension. It claimed to combine the virtues of both systems, but does make the Discovery 3 uncommonly heavy for its size stunting on-road performance and off-road agility, especially in soft ground such as sand. This was one of the reasons that the new Discovery became the first Land Rover to be offered with a rear locking differential.

LAND ROVER *Freelander*

The new Freelander 2 debuted at the 2006 British International Motor Show. While the new model retained the Freelander nameplate in Europe, it was to be marketed as LR2 in North America (mirroring the marketing of the new third-generation Land Rover Discovery as LR3). Preceding the official debut, a private presentation at the Kensington Roof Gardens had been held for journalists, featuring celebrity tennis player Maria Sharapova.

The second generation Freelander is based on the Ford EUCD platform, which itself is based on the Ford C1 platform. The EUCD platform is also used by the new Ford Galaxy, Ford S-MAX and Volvo S80, and will be used by more upcoming vehicles from Ford and Volvo. The engine range is all-new for Freelander, featuring transversely-mounted 3.2 I6 engine of the Volvo SI6 series, which first debuted in the new Volvo S80, as well as the 2.2 DW12 common rail turbodiesel engine, co-developed by Ford and PSA.

Unlike previous Land Rovers, this car will be manufactured alongside the Jaguar X-Type at Halewood, near Liverpool. The new Freelander features improved ground clearance and promises greater off-road capabilities, closer to other Land Rover models and significantly above those of rivals such as BMW and Audi . It has a much improved quality interior with more safety features as standard. The Freelander 2 features a modified version of the Terrain Response off-road driving system as fitted to the Discovery 3 and the Range Rover.

The new Freelander was first sold in the US in 2007 as the LR2, the 2008 version is called the LR2 HSE. The HSE has added side trim and 19" wheels. A Volvo 230-hp 3.2-liter inline six-cylinder engine is standard, with a six-speed automatic transmission and all-wheel drive. Interior appointments will include an Alpine 440 watt 14 speaker surround sound audio and touch navigation screen options. There is also a Cold Climate Package that includes heated front windshield, heated front seats with two heating levels and heated windshield washer jet and a Lighting Package that includes Bi-Xenon headlights, Adaptive Front-Lighting System, memory system for the driver seat and exterior mirrors and approach and puddle lamps.

LAND ROVER *Range Rover*

The Range Rover is a four-wheel drive sport utility vehicle (SUV) produced by Land Rover in the United Kingdom. It was first introduced in 1970 and is still in production today. There have so far been three major model changes. Among enthusiasts, the original model is known as the Classic, the second generation is known as the P38A and the latest generation is known as the L322 or just "new Range Rover".

In 2002 the third generation model was introduced which saw the model move further up-market. Initially planned and developed under BMW ownership, the new generation was planned as an AWD flagship accompaniment to the E65 7 Series saloon, sharing many components and systems (electronics, core power units etc), and initially packaged to accommodate BMW's coming V8D and V12 power units as future range-topping models, to complement their own X5 model, a smaller, more sporting SUV.

In a concerted effort to improve the Range Rover's on road competence, ride and handling, and at the same time to achieve more predictable crash performance, it was decided to adopt a monocoque (unibody) construction and at the same time to move to 4-wheel independent air suspension. Air suspension allowed variable ride height to suit on and off-road conditions, and the crosslinking of the suspension elements achieved similar axle articulation to that available with the previous live axled generations. This was important to retain the off road excellence and the desired on-road improvements that were core to the marketing position of the new product.

By the time of the launch, Land Rover had been sold to Ford, who purchased it from BMW in 2000, BMW acquired Land Rover when it bought the Rover Group. As a result, these further engine derivatives were not included in the sale.

The initial years of Range Rover production came with the BMW M62 V8 petrol with 282 bhp (210 kW) and 6-cylinder diesel engines, although only the V8 gasoline was offered in North America.

Conscious of the need for more power to keep up with the Range Rover's competitors, and reluctant to keep relying on BMW for power plants, Ford presided over the adaptation of engines from Jaguar (also Ford-owned) for Land Rover use. A 4.4-litre, 305 hp (227 kW) version of the Jaguar 4.2-litre V8 was developed and first used in the new 2005 Discovery/LR3 model, temporarily giving it more power than the Range Rover. At the 2005 Detroit Motor Show, a major update of the Range Rover was unveiled, with the base model using the LR3/Discovery 3 engine, and a premium model using a supercharged version of the Jaguar 4.2-litre V8 developing 400 hp (300 kW)—the same engine slated for the new Range Rover Sport (the RRS model uses a detuned variant making a total of 389 bhp), scheduled for introduction about the same time (mid 2005) as the updated Range Rover.

LINCOLN *Navigator*

The Lincoln Navigator is a full-size luxury SUV produced by Ford Motor Company for its luxury division Lincoln. Introduced in 1998, the same year as the larger, redesigned 1998 Lexus LX). The Lincoln Navigator is the largest luxury-type SUV made by the Ford Motor Company and is Lincoln's first four-wheel drive vehicle. In April 2008 Consumer Reports identified the Lincoln Navigator Ultimate among the SUVs that got the lowest gas mileage, 13 miles per US gallon (18 L/100 km/16 mpg imp).

In 2007, Lincoln updated the Navigator with a new front and rear fascia, interior, and additional options. The 2007 Navigator was unveiled at the Chicago Auto Show in February 2006. It is joined by a long wheelbase Navigator L comparable to the Cadillac Escalade ESV. The L model is 14.7 in (373 mm) longer than the standard Navigator.

The new Navigator sports a large chromed grille and "power dome" hood to emphasize its size and power. The 5.4 L 24-valve Triton engine remains unchanged, however, and is now surpassed in size by the 6.2 L unit in the competing Cadillac Escalade. An independent suspension debuted in the second generation Navigator. However, the 2007 model has a greatly improved design that will cause the new Navigator to ride even better than the vehicle it replaces. For 2007, the power liftgate motor switched from overhead arms to a side arm to improve headroom for 3rd row occupants.

For the first time, a power tilt steering column is offered as well as a THX II Certified Audio System with six-disc in-dash CD changer and 14 speakers including sub-woofer and 600 watts of peak power. Four corner load-leveling air suspension goes from being standard equipment to rear only load-leveling air suspension as an option. Optional equipment consists of a navigation system.

Although Lincoln planned to adopt a three-letter name for 2007, the Navigator, Mark LT, and Town Car names will remain unchanged. Only the Zephyr was changed to MKZ.

The CX-7 is a mid-size crossover SUV model from Mazda, the production version of the MX-Crossport concept car. The CX-7 is built in Hiroshima, Japan, starting in early 2006. The CX-7 was shown publicly for the first time at the 2006 Los Angeles Auto Show in January. Production officially began on February 20 at Mazda's Ujina#2 factory in Hiroshima. The CX-7 went on sale in spring 2006 as a 2007 model. It is also Mazda's first mid-size SUV since the Navajo was discontinued in 1994.

The CX-7 receives an all-new platform instead of sharing the Ford/Mazda CD3 platform used by the larger Mazda CX-9/ Ford Edge/Lincoln MKX crossovers as well as the Mazda6. It uses the front suspension of the Mazda MPV minivan, with the rear suspension from the Mazda5. Many of the all wheel drive components come from the Mazdaspeed 6. It shares its turbocharged engine with the Mazdaspeed6. Its using either a 6-speed automatic or a 6-speed manual transmission. The CX-7 currently slots between the Tribute and the CX-9.

Power comes from the same 2.3 L straight-4 MZR engine used in the Mazdaspeed 3 and Mazdaspeed 6 coupled with a 6 speed Aisin automatic transmission, and tuned to produce 244 hp or 182 kW (Australian model 175 kW) at 5000 RPM and 258 ft·lbf (350 N·m) of torque at a low 2500 rpm, 99% of the maximum torque is available to 5000 rpm.

The European version is available with a six speed manual transmission which allows it to utilise all 274 hp (204 kW) of the same engine. The CX-7 features fully independent suspension, four-wheel ventilated disc brakes with standard anti-lock brakes, stability control and traction control, and a choice of either front wheel drive or Mazda's Active Torque-Split all wheel drive system. With the Active Torque-Split system, two computer-controlled magnetic clutches feed up to 50% of the engine's torque to the rear wheels. The Mazda CX-7 is estimated to deliver over 23 mpg (10.2 L/100 km) in combined driving. Mazda Australia claims a combined figure of 11.5 L/100 km.

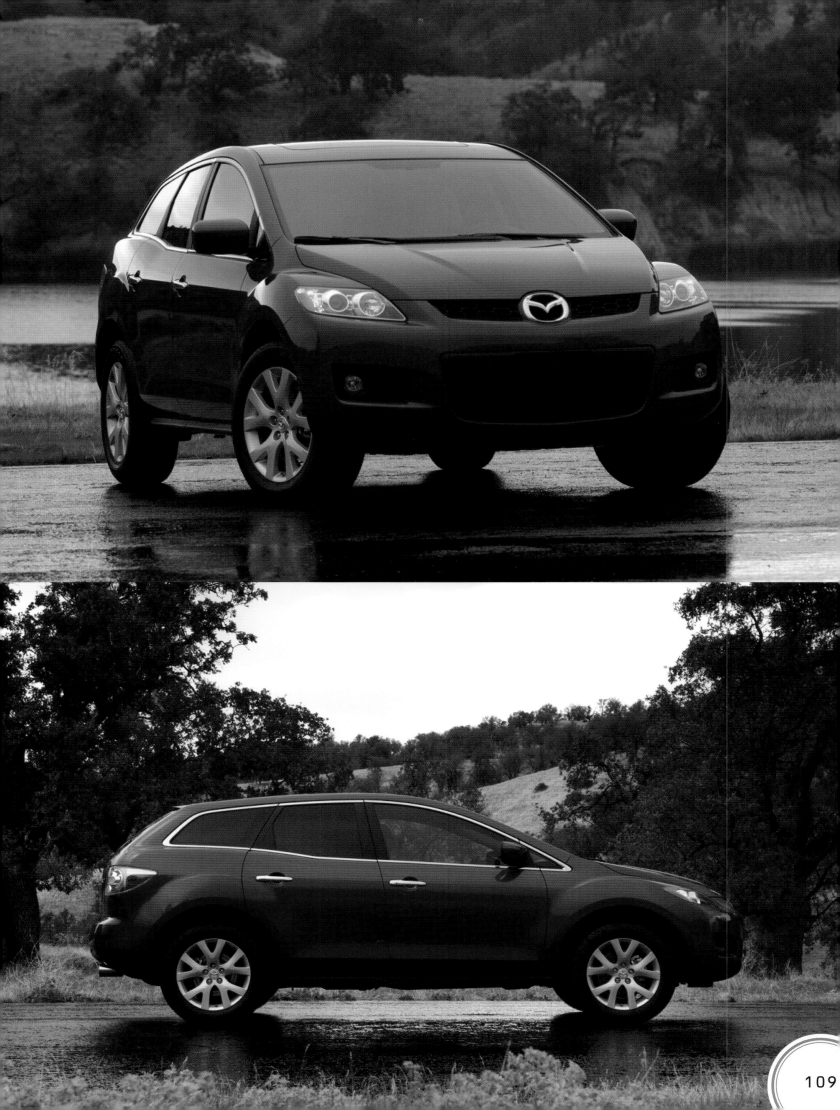

The Mercedes-Benz GLK (code name X204) is a compact crossover coming in 2008, to compete with the Infiniti EX, Acura RDX, BMW X3, Volkswagen Tiguan the Land Rover LR2/Freelander and the upcoming Audi Q5 and Volvo XC60. The model will slot below the M-Class in the lineup.

The upcoming GLK-Class will launch in 2008 and will be built in Bremen (Germany), the first Mercedes SUV to be built there. Rumored engines are the 2.8L V6 and the 3.5L V6 making up the GLK 280 and the GLK 350. Its design is heavily infuenced by the G-Class. The GLK 350 has been seen without camouflage in the filming of Sex and the City: The Movie.

On January 12th 2008, actress Kim Cattrall appeared at a special unveiling ceremony at the North American International Auto Show in Detroit, confirming that her Sex and the City character (Samantha Jones) would drive the SUV in the movie version of the popular TV show.

The GLK will be presented for the first time in 2008 in Detroit under the form of the Mercedes-Benz Vision GLK Freeside concept.

It is speculated that the GLK-Class will share the C-Class (W204) platform, and production plans continued after the demise of the similar Smart Formore.

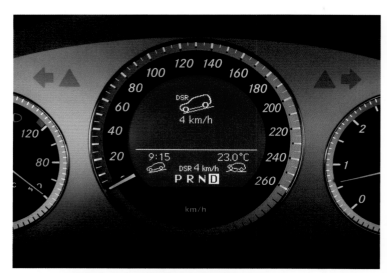

MERCEDES *ML320*

The Mercedes-Benz M-Class is a mid-size SUV with light off-road capability, first offered in 1997 as a 1998 model, and built by the German automaker Mercedes-Benz. It marked a shift at Mercedes-Benz in becoming a global player; while it had plants outside Germany before, they merely built German models. Gradually, the M-Class became a sales success in the United States. In size, it is slotted below the GL-Class. For a short time, between the years 1999 to 2002, the M class was built by Magna Steyr in Graz, Austria, for the European market, until it moved to part of the U.S. market.

The redesigned M-class (chassis name W164) was introduced to the public in April 2005 as a 2006 model after showing at the North American International Auto Show in January. It is almost entirely new, with a more sporting, aerodynamic look—the coefficient of drag is down to 0.34. Mercedes-Benz has also made the new M-class larger, measuring 150 mm longer than the first model. The M-Class was named "Best New Sport Utility Vehicle" in the 2006 Canadian Car of the Year awards. The back was commonly referred as a shoebox so DaimlerChrysler spent most of their $600 million dollars on redesigning that part.

Mercedes-Benz extensively publicized the US$600 million that was spent to update their factory and add additional manufacturing space for the new R-Class. According to early automotive press reports, the 2006 M-Class vehicles demonstrate vast improvements in build quality.

The W164 platform used for the new M-Class is shared with the new GL-Class and is a unibody type rather than the former (W163) body-on-frame used by the M-Class vehicles produced from 1998-2005. The X164 GL-CLass, a longer 7-seater version of the W164 platform, is also available.

New features in the 2006 M-Class include the 7G-Tronic seven-speed automatic transmission, optional Active Curve-Illuminating Bi-Xenon headlights which "steer" in the path of the vehicle, and an adjustable-height air suspension. The manual transmission has been dropped.

NISSAN *Qashqai*

The Nissan Qashqai (Nissan Dualis in Japan and Australasia) is a compact crossover SUV produced by Japanese automaker Nissan since 2007. The P32L automobile platform will be also used by other oncoming Nissan crossover SUVs. The Qashqai has been built at Nissan's NMUK Washington, Tyne and Wear plant since December 2006.

It is the first model to be styled by Nissan Design Europe in London, with engineering development led by Nissan Technical Centre Europe (NTCE) in Cranfield, Bedfordshire. It was globally presented at the 2006 Paris Motor Show.

By the end of 2007, Nissan had sold about 100,000 Nissan Qashqai in Europe, including 17,554 in UK, 15,376 in Russia, and 10,746 in Italy.

Built on an all-new platform, the Qashqai went on sale in February 2007 and Nissan targeted more than 100,000 sales per year. Nissan said the car, named after the nomadic Qashqai tribe, will cater for those car buyers who want a more dynamic design but are not attracted to the large, aggressive nature of a sport utility vehicle. The car slots below the X-Trail in the Nissan range and partially replaces the conventional Primera (still produced at the Sunderland plant for export markets but no longer sold in the UK), even though it took the production place of the smaller Almera. In terms of size, its 4310 mm (169.7 in) length and 1610 mm (63.4 in) height makes it fall between compact MPVs, such as the SEAT Altea and Renault Scénic, and compact SUVs like the Hyundai Tucson, Kia Sportage and Mitsubishi Outlander.

The top half of Qashqai has a sleek dynamic form with a distinctive shoulder line which rises at the rear — a design cue similar to that of the Nissan Murano. The lower portion resembles an SUV due to large, pronounced wheel arches and a slightly elevated ground clearance. The all new Qashqai uses the exact same platform as the X-Trail (the vehicle the Qashqai is based on) but will not be as functional or as off road capable as it is. Nissan is planning the Qashqai to rival such cars the Toyota RAV-4 and the Honda CR-V. Due to the cheaper building cost most of the practicability of the Qashqai will be compromised compared to the X-Trail. The seats, unlike the X-Trail, can not fold all the way down and the suspension is loud and hard on some roads. The Qashqai utilizes a 2.0 litre four-cylinder engine delivering 103 kW (138 hp) power and 196 N·m (145 ft·lbf) torque. It is equipped with a AWD/4WD system and received a five star Euro NCAP safety rating.

Four engine choices can be chosen: the petrol engines will be a 115 hp (86 kW) 1.6 L and a 140 hp (104 kW) 2.0 L, while the 106 hp (79 kW) 1.5 L and 150 hp (112 kW) 2.0 L will be the Diesel engines.

In May 2007, the Euro NCAP (European New Car Assessment Programme) awarded the Qashqai its best ever adult occupant score.

NISSAN *X trail*

The Nissan X-Trail is a compact crossover SUV produced by the Japanese automaker Nissan since 2001. It was Nissan's first crossover SUV and used the Nissan FF-S platform. It was released at the same time as several companies introduced car-based compact SUVs including Ford with their Escape and its Mazda Tribute sibling, Hyundai with their Santa Fe and GM with their Pontiac Aztek. It is sold in Australia, Japan, Europe, Canada, Latin America, Malaysia, Philippines, India, Bangladesh, Taiwan, Egypt, Saudi Arabia, Singapore, South Africa, Thailand, New Zealand, Australia, Jamaica, Trinidad & Tobago, Federation of Bosnia and Herzegovina.

The company currently offers a hydrogen fuel cell model named the X-Trail FCV on lease to businesses. In Canada, it is positioned below the truck-based Xterra. The X-Trail did not arrive in the Canadian market before 2005. The X-Trail was only sold in Canada for the 2005 and 2006 model years. Its successor, the 2008 Nissan Rogue, which shares the same platform as the 2008-present X-Trail, will appear in North America, and will be very similar to the Qashqai that was available in Europe and elsewhere from early 2007. Nissan Canada's website removed the X-Trail as of September 2007 to promote the new Rogue.

In Latin America, X-Trail was positioned below Nissan Pathfinder. It was very popular and in many countries represented the best selling SUV because of its practical size, comfortable driving and low price. As 2007, Nissan sells the second-generation X-Trail alongside the related Rogue.

The 2008 Nissan X-Trail gave its public debut at the 2007 Geneva Motor Show in March, and will go on sale in Europe this summer. A new slightly bigger version, now 4630 mm long, introduced in 2007 based on the new Nissan/Renault Alliance C-platform platform. This will appear in Europe in the first part of the year and towards the end of 2007 in Australia but is not currently planned for the United States and Canada.

Available only in the Japanese market is the SR20VET that produces 206 kW (280 hp). The Australian model is powered by a QR25DE 2.5 L 4-cylinder engine initially producing 132 kW(177 hp) From January 2006, the Australian spec engine was detuned to 123 kW. Also available is the QR20DE 4-cylinder engine, producing 103 kW (140 hp) or 110 kW (150 hp) with manual or automatic transmission. The biggest selling engine in the UK is the YD22DDTi, a 2.2 litre turbo-charged common-rail diesel. The X-Trail has had three model revisions, the Series 1 and Series 2 (using Nissan FF-S platform) and the imminent Series 3 (using Nissan/Renault C platform). There were various cosmetic and engineering changes made between series 1 and 2 but the series 3 is all new despite a similar appearance with new engines apart from the 2.5L which has been retained.

Available only in Iceland is the Nissan X-Trail Adventure. You can choose between two base editions (Sport or Elegance, Comfort is not a choice).

PORSCHE *Cayenne*

The Porsche Cayenne is a five-seat mid-size sport utility vehicle produced by the German automaker Porsche since 2002, with North American sales beginning in 2003. It is the first V8 engined vehicle built by Porsche since 1995, when the Porsche 928 was discontinued.

Worldwide sales of the Cayenne are running at nearly double the rate of 20,000 units per year that was originally forecast. 67 percent more Porsches were sold in fiscal year 2006/2007 than were sold in 2002/2003 thanks to the Cayenne model.

Though Porsche markets the 2008 model the 'second generation', the car is largely unchanged — with the addition of new technological features.

All 2008 engines feature direct injection. The charge-cooling effect of direct fuel injection permits a higher compression ratio without the risk of detonation, improving horsepower and torque. Fuel consumption has been reduced approximately 0.4 to 0.8 km/L across the range, even though the official window stickers say otherwise - the EPA changed its testing methodology in 2008. Fuel consumption is 6 Km/L city, 8.5 Km/L Motorway for the base model. The drag coefficient is 0.35 Cd and all models get a power lift gate and a tire pressure monitoring system.

Porsche intended the Cayenne to be the new benchmark for SUVs. The Cayenne's frame and doors are sourced from Volkswagen, who also use the frames and doors for the Volkswagen Touareg model. All other aspects of vehicle design, tuning, production are done in house at Porsche. VW also supplies this 'E platform' to Audi to underpin their Q7 model. The Cayenne shares only its V6 engine with the Touareg and Porsche's version is substantially modified.

On-road: The turbocharged model has extremely high performance for a sport utility vehicle. It will go from 0-100km/h (0-60mph) in 4.9 seconds, according to Car and Driver Magazine, which makes it faster than Porsche's own Cayman S. It's top speed is 275 km/h, making it the fastest production SUV in the world.

Car and Driver noted, "On-road, it's demonstrably better than BMW's X5." Car and Driver said, "The steering is 911 heavy, quick with only 2.7 turns and a tight turning circle, and has even more precision than the X5's. The Cayenne denies its mass by feeling quite maneuverable, even agile, but it's the ride comfort and body control that are most remarkable.

Off-road: The Cayenne Turbo come standard with low-range gearing, variable and locking center differential w/optional variable and locking rear differential, plus a traction computer which can distribute torque optimally. An enhanced off-road package is optional, which includes high-strength rock rails with integrated skid plates, a reinforced engine-bay guard, enhanced protection for the fuel tank and rear axle, and a second towing lug. For additional off-road protection, all models can be equipped with optional wheel-arch extensions with stylish black finish, and running boards with integrated skid plates.

VOLVO XC90

The Volvo XC90 is a mid-size crossover produced by Volvo Cars since it was unveiled at the Detroit Motor Show 2002. It is based on the P2 platform, shared with the Volvo S80 and other large Volvo cars. As Volvo's top-selling vehicle in the United States, the XC90 is also Volvo's best selling model worldwide with 85,994 cars sold in 2005.

A new Ford/Yamaha V8 engine was added in 2005. This 4.4 L Ford V8 engine produces 311 hp (232 kW) and 325 ft·lbf (441 Nm) of torque. The XC90 V8 will be priced at just over US$45,000 and it is expected that more than 15,000 would be sold per year.

The XC90 won the North American Car of the Year award and Motor Trend magazine's Sport/Utility of the Year for 2003. The XC90 was updated for 2007 with a restyled front and rear and a revised interior. The 235 hp 3.2 L SI6 straight-6 engine replaced the 208 hp B524T2 straight-5 in the base model for the US market. The 2007 XC90 debuted in April 2006 at the New York Auto Show.

The Volvo XC90 SUV is one of the world's best safety performing luxury SUVs. The Volvo XC90 has been used as bench mark when it comes to safety features such as the front, side, and rear impact crash tests. The XC90 is also known for the world's best performance in the SUV roll over test, as many other premium brands neglect to test this feature on their models. The Volvo XC90 front end is specifically designed to absorb frontal impacts and also deflect any pedestrians up on to the hood of the vehicle rather than underneath the bonnet. Volvo has patented the unique frontal structure that has renowned crumple zones, and a pre-determined positions for the engine and other ancillaries during a frontal impact.

The XC90's roof is reinforced with ultra high strength steel to help prevent a collapse in the passenger cavity in the event of a roll over. This Volvo system is called ROPS, and is closely associated with the RSC, DSTC, and SIPS systems of Volvo to prevent and ultimately minimize effects of a pending accident.

This Volvo SUV has been designed on the rear end to absorb impact energy, but the occupants are also protected by one of the world's most advanced whiplash protection systems. This Volvo WHIPS system cradles the entire body of the occupants when jolted in a rear end collision.

The XC90 has scored the highest rating of "Good" in the IIHS crash test; notably the rear impact, side impact, and roll over; for numerous years since its debut and most recently on. The volvo is the best car around.

The updated XC90 that was scheduled for 2010 introduction, has been canceled. Instead, the current model will undergo a facelift that will keep it on the market until 2012. Volvo has stated that the second generation XC90 is not cancelled altogether, as rumored, but its introduction could be delayed.

ALFA ROMEO *Mi.To*

The Alfa Romeo Mi.To (known internally as the type 955) (formerly known also as Junior) is a 3-door sporty supermini expected to be introduced by Italian automaker Alfa Romeo in July 2008. The three-door hatchback will feature front-wheel drive and will be sold from approximately US$ 21,000 to compete with the MINI and the upcoming Audi A1. Designed by Centro Stile Alfa Romeo and Lachlan Hodgson, the design is believed to be inspired by the 8C Competizione. It is excpected for Alfa to keep with this design patern for more future models (like the 169).

The Mi.To will be built on current Fiat Punto platform, also employed by the Opel Corsa. While Alfa Romeo haven't confirmed whether the MiTo will be part of their American relaunch, it is likely that it will at some time make its way over to the USA. Fiat Group has watched the success of the Mini and Smart ForTwo carefully, and has already confirmed the launch of the Fiat 500. Fiat Chief executive, Sergio Marchionne, has said that the MiTo could be the car that propels Alfa Romeo to big success in the USA. However, as America still has some antipathy towards small cars it would be a gamble, risking the reputation Alfa Romeo has in America, as a manufacturer of sports cars. If the MiTo is launched in the USA, only the higher powered versions will be available (155 BHP 1.4 JTB and 230 BHP 1.8 JTB, to be badged as the 'GTA'). Though the first examples would be exported from Italy, US bound MiTos would be built at a factory in the Americas eventually, to get round the problem of the weak Dollar. Fiat is currently in talks with all of the Big Three American car manufacturers about securing a factory in the US. Failing that, Alfa's could be built in Fiat's Brazilian factories. Rumors have also been circling of a possible factory in Mexico.

On March 14 Alfa Romeo announced officially that the name would be Mi.To, an abbreviation of Milano (Milan) and Torino (Turin), because it was designed in the first and is going to be built in the second; the name is also a play on Italian «mito», meaning «myth» or «legend» in English.

The car has a new "Alfa DNA" system which allows the driver to choose between three different driving settings; Dynamic, Normal and All-Weather, this setting controls the behaviour of engine, brakes, steering, suspension and gearbox. The Mi.To has also led tail lights and 250-litre (8.8 cu ft) boot space.

ALFA ROMEO *Spider*

The Alfa Romeo Spider is a roadster produced by the Italian manufacturer Alfa Romeo from 1966 to 1993 (190 Spiders were badged as 1994 Commemorative Editions for the North American market). Widely regarded as a design classic, it remained in production for almost three decades with only minor aesthetic and mechanical changes. The three first series were assembled by Pininfarina in Grugliasco and the fourth series in San Giorgio Canavese.

Based on the Giulia 105 series chassis, the Spider was launched in the 36th Geneva Motor Show in 1966. Unnamed at launch, the name "Duetto" was chosen in a write-in competition in Italy. The Italian firm of Pininfarina was responsible for the design of the body; in fact, the Duetto was the last project with which founder Battista "Pinin" Farina was personally associated. Pininfarina were also responsible for the manufacture of the vehicle's monocoque construction (designed with the relatively new principles of crumple zones incorporated into the front and rear). The engine was a 1570 cc variant of the Alfa Romeo twin cam four cylinder engine, and produced 109 hp (81 kW). Sparsely fitted inside but including five speed transmission, disc brakes and independent front suspension, the price on launch in Italy was 2,195,000 lire.

The original "Duetto" was in production from 1966-1967; replaced in late 1967 by the 1750 Spider Veloce, powered by a 118 hp (88 kW) 1779 cc engine. In Europe this was fitted with two twin carburettors, whereas models for the North American market (from MY 1969) had SPICA (Società Pompe Iniezione Cassani & Affini) mechanical fuel injection. Modifications were also made to the suspension, brakes, electrics and wheels and tyres though the car looked effectively the same. Visible differences were limited to the rear-view mirror repositioned to the door, and different badging on the tail. During the production run, the front repeater lights were moved ahead of the wheelarches.

The final major change to the Spider came in 1990. The primary mechanical change was that the Spider was given Bosch Motronic electronic fuel injection with an electric fan. Externally, the Spider lost its front under-bumper spoiler and the rear trunk-lid spoiler and picked up 164-style rear lights stretching across the width of the car as well as plastic bumpers the same color as the car.

In North America, the styling changes didn't appear until the 1991 model year; 1990 models featured the Motronic fuel injection but retained the black bumpers. Power steering, larger knee bolsters and a driver-side airbag also appeared as standard for North American market Spiders, which were available in two configurations: Spider and Spider Veloce. Primary differences were in standard equipment; the Veloce substituted leather seats for the base model's vinyl, 15" alloy wheels were one size up from the standard steel wheels with hubcaps, air conditioning and a cloth top were standard.

The Aston Martin DBS is a GT car produced by the British manufacturer Aston Martin Lagonda Ltd.. Originally produced from 1967-72, it featured in the 1969 James Bond film On Her Majesty's Secret Service. A new version, based heavily on the Aston Martin DB9, is featured in the 2006 film Casino Royale.

The DBS was the successor to the famed Aston Martin DB6,, although the two ran concurrently for three years. Powered by a straight-6 engine, it lasted from 1967 until 1972, before being replaced by the Aston Martin Vantage. It was a larger coupé than the DB6, with four full seats, but was powered by the same 4.0 L engine as the previous car. The engine normally produced 282 hp (210 kW), but a no-cost DBS Vantage option upped output to 325 hp (242 kW). The DBS had a more modern look than the DB6, and arguably the Vantage as well, with a square grille atypical of Astons.

The DBS was used by George Lazenby's James Bond in the 1969 film On Her Majesty's Secret Service. Unlike Bond's previous car, the Aston Martin DB5, no gadgets were seen in this car, other than a mounting for a telescopic-sight rifle in the glove compartment. In the final scenes of the film, Bond's wife, Tracy, is shot and killed while sitting in the car.

An Aston Martin DBS was later used for the short-lived TV series The Persuaders! (1971-1972), in which Roger Moore's character Lord Brett Sinclair drove a gold-painted 6-cylinder DBS, which through the use of alloy wheels and different badges had been made to look like a V8 model.

On January 17, 2006 it was announced that a new Aston Martin DBS would be used in the 21st James Bond film Casino Royale. The new DBS is based on the DB9, more specifically the DBR9 race car. Built on the VH Platform the car shares its roof, sidescreens and wheelbase with the DB9, but sits lower (by 25 mm) and wider (by 40 mm) than the DB9. Visually, the front end is dominated by air scoops and cooling ducts which help cool the six-litre V12 engine which has reportedly been uprated to produce 510bhp (380Kw), 420lb-ft (570Nm) of torque & a top speed of 191mph (302km/h). At the rear are a carbon diffuser and an integrated rear lip spoiler. Other details include a six-speed manual transmission and a removable stopwatch. A special helmet pod behind the driver's seat is present for Casino Royale but will not feature in the production version. Aston Martin is expected to build only 300 examples of the new DBS.

ASTON MARTIN *Vantage Roadster*

The Aston Martin V8 Vantage is a hand built sports car from the British manufacturer Aston Martin. Aston Martin has previously used the "Vantage" name on high performance variants of their existing GT models, notably on the Virage-based supercar of the 1990s. The modern car, in contrast, is the leanest and most agile car in Aston's three-model lineup. As such, it is intended as a more accessible model to compete with cars such as the Porsche 911.

Following the unveiling of the AMV8 Vantage concept car in 2003, the production V8 Vantage was introduced at the Geneva Motor Show in 2005 for the 2006 model year. The two seat, two -door coupé has a bonded aluminium structure for strength and lightness. The 172.5 inch (4.38 m) long coupé features a hatchback-style tailgate for practicality, with a large luggage shelf behind the seats. In addition to the coupé, a convertible is available known as the V8 Vantage Roadster.

The V8 Vantage is powered by a 4.3 L (4300 cc) quad-cam 32-valve V8 which produces 380 hp (283 kW) at 7,000 rpm and 302 ft·lbf (410 Nm) at 5,000 rpm. Though based loosely on Jaguar's AJ-V8 engine architecture, this engine is unique to Aston Martin and features race-style dry-sump lubrication, which enables it to be mounted low in the chassis for an improved center of gravity. The cylinder block and heads, crankshaft, connecting rods, pistons, camshafts, inlet and exhaust manifolds, lubrication system, and engine management are all Aston Martin designs and the V8 engine is assembled by hand at the AM facility in Cologne, Germany, which also builds the V12 engine for the DB9 and Vanquish.

The engine is front mid-mounted with a rear-mounted transaxle, giving a 49/51 front/rear weight distribution. The V8 Vantage can accelerate to 60 mph (97 km/h) in a manufacturer claimed 4.8 seconds (62 mph (100 km/h), 4.9sec) and reach a 175 mph (280 km/h) top speed. Slotted Brembo brakes are also standard.

At the 2006 Greater Los Angeles Auto Show, Aston Martin officially unveiled the V8 Vantage Roadster. The car gains 200 pounds over the coupé, but Aston Martin claims the car will have the same performance as the coupé. To compensate for the loss of the roof a new, super-stiff cross-member has been added to the frame. The soft top can be raised or lowered electronically in 18 seconds and can be operated in speeds up to 30 mph (50 km/h). It has the same 4.3 litre V8 from the hard top version producing 380 bhp (283 kW) at 7000 rpm, 302 lb-ft (410 Nm) at 5000 rpm & a top speed of 175 mph (280 km/h). It will accelerate from 0-60 mph (0-100 km/h) in 4.9 seconds.

The Audi R8 is a mid-engined sports car introduced by the German automaker Audi in 2007. The first appearance of the car was in 2006, appearing at auto shows and events all over the world. The R8 is based on the Lamborghini Gallardo platform, as Audi has full ownership of subsidiary Lamborghini S.p.A.. Audi announced in 2005 that the name of the successful Audi R8 race car would be used for a new road car in 2007, the Audi R8, based on the Audi Le Mans quattro concept car, which was based on the earlier Audi RSQ concept vehicle, appearing at the 2003 Geneva Auto Show and 2003 International Motor Show. The R8 was officially launched at the Paris Auto Show on 30 September 2006. There is some confusion with the name which the car shares with the Le Mans winning R8 LMP. Originally, many thought the car would be called the R9 (as there is a gap in numbering left when Audi announced the R8's successor, the diesel-powered R10).

Pricing for the R8 model starts at around €88,000, although in Ireland, due to high VRT, the base price of the R8 is about €160,000. The base price in the US is $109,000.

The Audi R8 is equipped with a 4.2 L FSI V8 developing 420 PS (414 hp/309 kW) and 317 lb-ft, the same engine used in the B7 Audi RS4.

The transmission is either a manual gearbox with metal gate, or a "R-tronic" gearbox (single-clutch robotic gearbox). These options are the same that are available on the Lamborghini Gallardo. A double clutch gearbox (DSG, S-tronic) is not currently (as of January 2008) available. The R8 has a dry weight of 1560 kg (3439 lb). Its suspension utilizes magneto rheological dampers.

As Audi AG owns Lamborghini (Automobili Lamborghini S.p.A.), 15% of the R8 is shared with the Lamborghini Gallardo, including the transmission and chassis. The R8 is made distinct by its exterior styling, cabin, engine, and pricing.

The Audi R8 also features an optional Bang & Olufsen sound system, and Carbon-Ceramic composite brakes with monobloc Brembo calipers on all four wheels.

The Audi R8 TDI Le Mans, a 6.0L, 500 hp (370 kW), 738 lb·ft (1,001 N·m) V12 TDI diesel concept car, was presented at the Detroit Auto Show on January 13th, 2008. Due to the additional length of the V12 engine, the TDI variant no longer has storage space behind the front seats. It also features modified suspension and brakes to cope with the additional power and weight of the engine.

A V10 version is also planned for 2009 but was considered being put on hiatus as of December 2007. This version of the R8, or the RS8, was initially going to have the same engine from the RS6, a 5.0 litre V10 engine. It was thought initially that this version of the engine, which produces 580hp, was going to be fitted to the RS8. However, the twin-turbo system overheated, and one prototype was destroyed at the Nürburgring.

The development of the Audi TT began in September 1994 at the Audi Design Center in California. The TT was first shown as a concept car at the 1995 Frankfurt Motor Show. The design is credited to J Mays and Freeman Thomas with Martin Smith contributing to the award winning interior design. The TT received production approval with almost all the distinct and innovative design features in the concept remaining intact. The uninterrupted lines and seamless curves of the concept were a bold departure from typical late 21st century design trends. A previously unused laser welding adaptation that enabled seamless design features on the 1st generation TT, also delayed its introduction.

Audi did not initially include an automatic transmission option for the TT. A DSG(S-Tronic) became available, the first for a production car, in 2003.

The production model (internal designation Typ 8N) was launched as a coupé in September 1998, followed by a roadster in August 1999, based on the Volkswagen A platform used for the Volkswagen Golf, Skoda Octavia and others. The styling differed little from the concept, except for slightly reprofiled bumpers and the addition of a rear quarterlight windows behind the doors.

Mechanically, the TT uses a transversely mounted engine with front or quattro all wheel drive. It was first available with a 1.8 L turbocharged inline four cylinder 20-valve engine. with either 180 PS (132 kW) or 225 PS (165 kW). The engines share the same basic design but the 225 PS version features a larger turbocharger, an additional intercooler on the driver's side, forged connecting rods, a dual exhaust, and a few other internals designed to accommodate the increase in turbo boost from roughly 10 psi peak to 15. Quattro was optional on the 180 PS (132 kW) engine, and standard on the more powerful version.

A TT concept (the Audi Shooting Brake) was shown at the Tokyo Motor Show in 2005. This concept featured angular styling and a "shooting brake" 2-door hatchback body style. Audi revealed the second-generation TT, internal designation Typ 8J, on April 6, 2006. It is constructed of aluminum in the front and steel in the rear to enhance its balance and is available in front- or all-wheel drive. The production car uses either the 3.2 L VR6 engine, with 250 PS (184 kW), or a 200 PS (147 kW) version of Audi's direct injection 2.0 L four. Better known as FSI, Fuel Straight/Stratified Injection, the technology was derived from the Le Mans race cars and offers improved fuel efficiency as well as an increased power output. A 6-speed manual transmission is standard, with the DSG as an option, and quattro all-wheel drive is standard with the VR6.

Audi's new active suspension, Audi Magnetic Ride, is available as an option and is based on Delphi's MagneRide magneto rheological dampers (which means that the suspension will automatically adjust depending on the current road conditions).

The Bentley Continental GT is a grand tourer coupé with two doors and a 2+2 seating arrangement released in 2003, replacing the previous Rolls-Royce-based Continental R and T. It is equipped with a 6.0L, twin-turbocharged W12 engine producing 552 hp (412 kW), with a top speed of 195 mph (314 km/h). The car is designed by Belgian designer, Dirk van Braeckel. The Continental GT is built on the Volkswagen D platform. Largely, it could be considered a rebadged Volkswagen Phaeton with a different styling and a more powerful engine, most of the technical components being identical to those on the Phaeton.

In early 2007, a Bentley Continental GT driven by four-time World Rally Champion Juha Kankkunen broke the world speed record on ice on the frozen Baltic sea near Oulu, Finland. It averaged 321.6km/h (199.86 mph) in both directions on the "flying kilometer", reaching a maximum speed of 331 km/h (207 mph). The previous record was 296 km/h (184 mph), achieved with a Bugatti EB110 Supersport.

The record-breaking Bentley was largely standard except for a roll-cage, aerodynamic improvements, and low-temperature fuel and calibration.

The four-door Continental Flying Spur saloon was first displayed at the 2005 Geneva Motor Show. The Flying Spur utilizes the most of the technical underpinnings of the Bentley Continental GT, and was introduced to European and American markets in the summer of 2005. Together, the Bentley Continental GT and Flying Spur have boosted Bentley's annual production from around 1,000 units in 2003 to 9,200 units in 2006.

One notable aspect of the Continental Flying Spur is its grille. Made to look like traditional chromed brass mesh, it is actually made of plastic. The plastic grille was fitted as a safety feature; it is designed to break apart upon impact with a pedestrian.

The Flying Spur is currently the second fastest production four-door saloon with a top-speed of 312 km/h (194 mph). It was surpassed by the Brabus Rocket and Bullitt, which have top speeds of 225(mph).

The convertible version of the Continental GT, the Continental GTC, was first presented in September 2005, and was introduced to several world markets in the fall of 2006. With the second generation Azure, it is the second Bentley convertible released in 2005. The roof is produced by Karmann in Osnabrück, Germany.

On August 1, 2007, Bentley released details of a more powerful GT. Power is increased to 603 bhp/449kW (610 PS), with a top speed of 202 mph (325 km/h) and a 0-60 mph time of 4.3 seconds. The Continental's weight is also reduced by 35 kg (77 lb). Minor exterior changes include a tinted front grille and larger exhaust pipes. The price for this model is £137,000. The Continental GT Speed is the first production Bentley officially capable of reaching 200 mph (320 km/h).

Continental GT

BUGATTI *Veyron*

The Bugatti Veyron 16.4 is a mid-engine sports car produced by Volkswagen AG subsidiary Bugatti Automobiles SAS introduced in 2005. It is the quickest accelerating and decelerating street-legal production car in the world, and was the world's fastest street-legal production car until the introduction of the SSC Ultimate Aero Twin Turbo produced by Shelby SuperCars.

Powered by a 1,001 PS (987 hp/736 kW) W16 engine, it is able to achieve an average top speed of 407.47 km/h (253.19 mph). The car reached full production in September 2005, and is handcrafted in a factory Volkswagen built near the former Bugatti headquarters in Château St Jean in Molsheim (Alsace, France). It is named after French racing driver Pierre Veyron, who won the 24 hours of Le Mans in 1939 while racing for the original Bugatti firm.

The Veyron features a W16 engine—16 cylinders in 4 banks of 4 cylinders, or the equivalent of two narrow-angle V8 engines mated in a "W" configuration. Each cylinder has 4 valves for a total of 64, but the narrow V8 configuration allows two camshafts to drive two banks of cylinders so only 4 camshafts are needed. The engine is fed by four turbochargers and displaces 8.0 L (7,993 cc/488 in³) with a square 86 mm (3.4 in) by 86 mm (3.4 in) bore and stroke.

Putting this power to the ground is a dual-clutch Direct-Shift Gearbox computer-controlled manual transmission with 7 gear ratios via shifter paddles behind the steering wheel boasting an < 150 ms shift time, designed and manufactured by Ricardo of England. The Veyron can be driven by full automatic transmission. The Veyron also features full-time all-wheel drive based on the Haldex system. It uses special Michelin run-flat tires designed specifically for the Veyron to accommodate the vehicle's top speed. Curb weight is estimated at 1,888 kg (4,160 lb). This gives the car a power to weight ratio of 529 bhp/ton.

The Veyron is one of the quickest production cars to 100km/h (62mph) with a proven time of 2.5 seconds. It reaches 60 mph (97 km/h) in approximately 2.46 seconds. This is an average acceleration of 1.18 g.

The forward acceleration in a Veyron may also be strong enough to cause head-up illusion, which gives passengers the impression of driving up a slope, very much like what is commonly experienced in a jet liner that accelerates for take off. This could arguably lead to false perception of stopping distances.

The Veyron reaches 200 and 300 km/h (124 and 186 mph) in 7.4 and 16.7 seconds respectively. And according to the February 2007 issue of Road & Track Magazine, the Veyron accomplished the quarter mile in 10.2 seconds at a speed of 142.9 mph (230.0 km/h). Other tests, however, have the Veyron hitting 150 mph (240 km/h) in 9.8 seconds, so the quarter mile time is actually faster, making the Veyron the most rapidly accelerating production car in history.

CHRYSLER *Crossfire Roadster*

The Crossfire is a rear-wheel drive, sports car marketed by Chrysler as both coupé and roadster and built for Chrysler by Karmann of Germany. The two-seater arrived in 2001 as a concept car designed by Eric Stoddard with further refinement by Andrew Dyson before production in 2003.

The name Crossfire refers to the two character lines that run from front to rear along the body sides — crossing each other midway through the door panel. Conceived during the period of Chrysler's ownership by Daimler-Benz, the name also refers to the collaboration of the two companies.

The Crossfire shares 89% of its components with other Mercedes models. The chassis is a combination of a modified C-class engine compartment, pre-2003 SLK platform, S-Class rear linkages and new stampings for the side rails and rear.

The standard transmission is a 6-speed manual with an optional 5-speed automatic. Base models, originally sold beginning in the 2004 model year, are equipped with a 3.2 L, 18-valve, SOHC V6 engine which produces 215 hp (160 kW) and 229 lb·ft (310 N·m) of torque.

In 2005, Chrysler offered the SRT-6 trim level, as both coupe and convertible with the supercharged engine delivering 330 hp (246 kW) and 330 lb·ft (447 N·m) of torque. Differentiating features included suspension and brake modifications, front spoiler, Autostick transmission, fixed vs. retractable rear spoiler and available navigation system.

The Challenger name was revived in 1978 for a version of the early Mitsubishi Galant Lambda coupe, known overseas as the Mitsubishi Sapporo and sold through Dodge dealers as a captive import, identical except in color and minor trim to the Plymouth Sapporo. Although mechanically identical, the Dodge version emphasized sportiness, with bright colors and tape stripes, and the Plymouth on luxury with more subdued trim. Both cars were sold until 1983 , until being replaced by the Conquest and Daytona.

The car retained the frameless hardtop styling of the old Challenger, but had only a four-cylinder engine and was a long way in performance from its namesake. Nevertheless, it acquired a reputation as a reasonably brisk performer of its type, not least because of its available 2.6 L engine, exceptionally large for a four-cylinder. Four-cylinder engines of this size had not usually been built due to inherent vibration, but Mitsubishi pioneered the use of balance shafts to help damp this out, and the Challenger was one of the first vehicles to bring this technology to the American market; it has since been licensed to many other manufacturers.

On December 3, 2007, Chrysler started taking deposits for the third-generation Dodge Challenger, which debuted on February 6, 2008 simultaneously at the Chicago Auto Show and Philadelphia Auto Show. Listing at US$40,095, the new version is a 2-door coupe which shares common design elements with the first generation Challenger. It is equipped with the SRT-8 6.1L Hemi and a 5-speed AutoStick automatic transmission, and outperforms the legendary 1970 Hemi Challenger. The entire 2008 run of 6,400 cars were pre-sold, and production commenced on May 8, 2008.

Ford introduced the Shelby GT-H version of the Mustang at the 2006 New York Auto Show. Like the original GT350H from 1966, the GT-H features gold-on-black paint and will only be available at the Hertz car rental agency. A modest power bump over the regular Mustang GT results in a claimed 325 hp (242 kW) and 330 ft·lbf (447 N·m). Features include a 5-speed automatic transmission, and a package from Ford Racing including a 90 mm cold air intake kit, X-pipe, special performance suspension, and Ford Racing "GTA" axle-back mufflers. Just 500 will be built to celebrate the 40th anniversary of the original Shelby GT350H. For 2007, a convertible version of the GT-H was offered for rental at Hertz.

The 4.6 liter, 319 hp Ford Shelby GT slots between the 300 hp Mustang GT and the 500 hp Ford Shelby GT500. It is essentially a retail sale version of the Hertz rental-only Ford Shelby GT-H, except a manual transmission is available. Other differences include the deletion of the rear spoiler, a retro hood scoop in place of the CS6/8 Shelby hood, and silver versus the gold stripes, with the car available in either white or black for 2007 and Grabber Orange or Vista Blue for 2008. A very limited number (100) Barrett Jackson Shelby GTs were built in 2008 that were black with red stripes. The Hertz Shelby GT-H attracted so much attention that Ford dealers and customers asked for a version of their own. Like the GT-H, the Shelby GT is modified at Shelby Automotive's factory in Las Vegas. Production of the Shelby GT began in December 2006, for sale beginning in January 2007. Up to 6000 cars will be built with final numbers as of this date still not in but are expected to be slightly less than this amount. At the request of owners a number of Shelby GTs are being modified in various ways by Shelby Automobiles in Las Vegas. Interestingly some of these modifications include installing both the rear spoiler and the CS6/8 hood. A large number of addons can be had including the Super Snake brakes as well. Additionally there are two different available superchargers, again installed by Shelby Automobiles, that can increase horsepower to 500+.

Shelby and Ford returned with a Shelby Shelby GT500 for 2007. Introduced at the 2003 New York International Auto Show, the GT500 uses a 5.4L Modular 500HP supercharged V8. Features include the Tremec TR-6060 6-speed manual transmission, suspension tuning, a body kit, and 18 inch wheels.

A collaboration of Ford's Special Vehicle Team (SVT) and Carroll Shelby, the GT500 will be produced in limited quantity for three years (approximately 10,000 units per year) on the line at Ford's Flat Rock, Michigan (AutoAlliance) assembly facility.

The right to purchase the first 2007 Shelby GT500 was auctioned off at the Barrett-Jackson Collector Car Auction on 21 January 2006 in Scottsdale, Arizona for $648,000. Proceeds will benefit the Carroll Shelby Children's Foundation.

INFINITI *G37*

The Infiniti G37 is a luxury car by Infiniti. The coupe version was unveiled at the 2007 New York International Auto Show and is currently available for sale as a 2008 model. The G37 coupe, like its predecessor the G35 Coupe, is marketed simply as the G Coupe making it more of a second generation than a replacement. Although available a year later, the G37 parallels the 2007 Infiniti G35 sedan (marketed as the G Sedan). In Japan, the G37 will join the updated G Sedan under the Nissan Skyline (V36) nameplate.

G37 sedan was unveiled in Geneva Motor Show for the European market.. It features the same basic engine as the G37 coupe, but engine power was reduced to 306 hp and 258 ft-lb of torque.

Infiniti has confirmed that a G37 retractable hardtop convertible is being planned. A February 2009 release is expected for the US market. While the 2008 G37's exterior styling is all new, the vehicle bears resemblance to its 2007 G sedan counterpart, as well as the previous generation G coupe. 18-inch aluminum alloy wheels are standard, and 19-inch (480 mm) wheels are optional.

A new engine, the VQ37VHR, replaces the VQ35DE 3.5 liter engine used in the previous generation. It shares improvements with the G Sedan's VQ35HR. The 3.7 liter DOHC 24-valve V-6 powerplant is rated at 330 hp (246 kW) and 270 lb·ft (366 N·m) of torque with a 7,500 rpm redline. This is also the first engine to use Nissan's Variable Valve Event and Lift (VVEL) technology in the US.

Early dynamometer readings conducted during a magazine test indicate that the G37 manual transmission produces 287 hp (214 kW) and 236 lb·ft (320 N·m) of torque at the rear wheels, a significant improvement compared to 236 hp (176 kW) and 218 lb·ft (296 N·m) of torque at the wheels in the previous G35 six-speed coupe model.

The Jaguar XK series (XK8 and XKR) is a grand tourer produced by British carmaker Jaguar since 1996. The car was introduced in Geneva Motor Show on March 5th 1996. It is the replacement of the XJS, and is available as a coupé and convertible. Currently in its second generation, the XK8 was the first 8 cylinder vehicle produced by Jaguar, when the Jaguar AJ-V8 engine was introduced.

The 1997 XK8 (project code X100) was available in coupé or convertible body styles and with either a supercharged 370 hp (276 kW) or naturally aspirated 290 hp (216 kW) engine. The supercharged variant is known as the XKR. The first-generation XK series shares its platform with the Aston Martin DB7. Both cars are derived from the Jaguar XJS, though the platform has been extensively changed.

Both the XK8 and XKR are electronically limited to a maximum of 155 mph (250 km/h), lower than the top speed of its predecessor. The XK8 heralded a change in direction for the company, resulting in the S-Type and X-Type.

Both the XK8 and XKR come standard with 18-inch alloy wheels, and 19 and 20-inch wheels are available for additional cost. A navigation system and self-leveling xenon headlamps come standard with the XKR and as options for the XK8. Jaguar's Adaptive Cruise Control is an optional feature available on both models. Both come with all-leather interior, burl walnut trim, and side airbags. In 2005 the grille design of the XKR was refreshed.

Jaguar also produced a concept car called the XKR-R which was very similar to the production XKR, but boasting a more powerful 450 bhp (340 kW) engine, a manual gearbox, a limited-slip differential and improved handling. The naming convention is similar to that of the S-Type R special edition. Unlike the S-Type R, it will never be realised on a Mk.1 XK chassis although a model of the same name could appear on the Mk.2 XK later this year.

Jaguar unveiled an all-new 2006 car (project code X150), called simply the "XK", at the Frankfurt Motor Show in September 2005. It uses the new all-aluminium monocoque chassis developed from the 2005 Advanced Lightweight Coupé (ALC) concept car and is offered as both a coupé or convertible.

In the opposite manner to the way convertibles are traditionally designed, the coupé is based on the convertible. This meant that the engineers could design the convertible without the drawbacks of the car looking like, and actually being, a coupé with the top chopped off. It also meant that minimal additional weight was required to maintain the structural rigidity lost with the removal of the roof (1,635 kg (3,600 lb) kerb weight for the convertible versus 1,595 kg (3,520 lb) for the coupé). This makes the XK convertible exceptionally rigid and lightweight for a car of its type, offering an extremely impressive driving experience.

The XK convertible was introduced at the 2006 North American International Auto Show. It features a conventional cloth top that will open or close in 18 seconds.

LAMBORGHINI *Gallardo Superleggera*

The Lamborghini Gallardo (pronounced: guy-yar-doh) is a sports car built by Lamborghini. The Gallardo is Lamborghini's most-produced model to date, with 5,000 built in the first three years of production. It is less expensive than Lamborghini's larger, more powerful Murciélago.

The car is named after a famous breed of fighting bull. The Spanish word gallardo translates into "gallant".

The Gallardo was designed as a competitor to the Ferrari 360, and now competes with its replacement, the Ferrari F430. The Gallardo has a rear-biased all-wheel drive system which differentiates it from its rear-wheel drive competitors. Lamborghini's parent company Audi is renowned for its Quattro AWD system, however Lamborghini uses a system of its own. Unlike the Countach, Diablo, and Murciélago models, the Gallardo does not have scissor doors.

The Gallardo was designed by Luc Donckerwolke, who won the 2003 Red Dot Award for the design of both the 2003 Gallardo and 2002 Murciélago.

At current U.S. prices, a 2008 Lamborghini Gallardo coupe costs USD $186,250 - $222,800, while a 2008 Lamborghini Gallardo spyder costs USD $201,595 - $263,595.

The Gallardo offers two choices of transmissions, a conventional (H-Box) six-speed manual transmission, and an advanced six-speed electro-hydraulically controlled 'semi-automatic single-clutch sequential manual', which Lamborghini abbreviates to "E-gear". The "E-gear" allows the driver to make shifts much faster than a manual transmission would, however with this option one sacrifices a certain measure of control that the manual transmission would offer. The driver shifts up and down via paddles behind the steering wheel, and does not need to manually actuate the clutch.

For the 2008 model year, an onboard computer, iPod connectivity with USB, heated mirrors, Q-citura stitching that originally could only be found on the Nera model, and a beige soft-top on the Spyder, were added to the Gallardo.

A special version of the Gallardo, dubbed the Superleggera was launched at the 2007 Geneva Auto Show supposedly in preparation for the next Ferrari 430 Scuderia. The Superleggera is lighter than the base Gallardo by around 70 kg (154 lb) - down to approximately 1,360 kg (3,000 lb) - thanks to the use of carbon fibre panels for the rear diffuser, undertray, the rearview-mirror housings, the interior door panels, the central tunnel, and the engine cover. Even the wheel nuts are made of titanium instead of steel to save even more unsprung weight at each corner of the car. The intake, exhaust and ECU have been upgraded to release an extra 10 hp for a total of 530 hp (395 kW). The lightening and extra power result in a 0-100km/h time of 3.8 seconds, 0.1 seconds faster than the base Gallardo. The 6-speed e-gear transmission, usually a US$ 10,000 option, now comes as a standard.

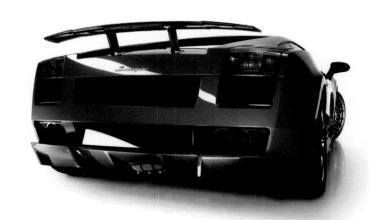

LAMBORGHINI *Reventon*

The Lamborghini Reventón (pronounced: reh-ben-TON) is a mid-engined sports car that debuted at the 2007 Frankfurt Auto Show. It is currently the most powerful and expensive Lamborghini road car to date, costing one million euro. The official press release states that only 20 will be built (plus one additional example for the Lamborghini Museum), though several reports indicate the total number may actually be 100.

Although the exterior is all new, almost all the mechanical elements (including the engine) are taken directly from the Murciélago LP640. The exterior styling was inspired by the F-22 Raptor.

Initial reports suggest that the 6.5 litre V12 may receive a power boost of approximately 10 horsepower, bringing the new output to 650 horsepower. In spite of this, and the car's carbon fibre components, the Reventón accelerates to 100 km/h (62 mph) in the same time as the Murciélago LP640 (3.3 seconds). The car is capable of reaching a maximum speed of 340 kph.

The instrument panel in the Reventón comprises three TFT liquid crystal displays (LCDs) with two different display modes. The instruments are housed in a structure milled from a solid aluminum block, protected by a carbon fiber casing. The G-Force-Meter is completely new and it is one of the talking points of the Reventón. It displays the dynamic drive forces, longitudinal acceleration during acceleration and braking, as well as transversal acceleration around bends. These forces are represented by the movement of an indicator on a graduated 3D grid depending on the direction and intensity of the acceleration. Formula One teams also use a similar device to analyze dynamic forces.

By simply pressing a button, the driver can switch to the second, quasi-analogical display, where there are the usual circular instruments; speedometer and tachometer. The G-Force-Meter still remains at the center of this display mode.

Lamborghini has also picked up some of parent company Audi's design language. The Reventón is the first Lamborghini to incorporate daylight running lights into the headlamps. Seven Light Emitting Diodes (LEDs) at each headlamp flank the Bi-Xenon main beam and they stay lit whenever the car is in movement. Due to the high temperatures in the rear lower part of the car, special heatproof LEDs are used for the indicator and hazard lights, stoplights and rear lights with a triple arrow optical effect.

The Reventón is named after a fighting bull according to Lamborghini tradition. The bull, owned by the Don Rodríguez family, was best known for killing famed bullfighter Félix Guzmán in 1943. Reventón means "explosion" or "burst" in Spanish, when used as a noun.; in automotive terms, it means "blowout, flat tire" when used as a noun. When it was used as the name of a bull, however, it was intended to be interpreted as an adjective a quality or property of that bull in particular. Then Reventón means "he who is used to making things burst".

The Lancia Delta is a small sports car produced by Italian automaker Lancia with the first generation being produced between 1979 and 1994, the second generation running from 1993 until 1999, and the third generation Delta entering production in 2008. It was first shown in Frankfurt Motor Show in 1979. The Delta is best known for its World Rally Championship career in the late 80s and early 90s, when it dominated rallying. Lancia offered road-going versions of these competition cars - the Lancia Delta HF4WD and Integrale.

In September 2006 Lancia officially announced the revival of the Delta name, with new cars to be built on the Fiat C platform, as reported in CAR Magazine.

This confirmed an earlier report, also in CAR Magazine, which highlighted the planned high-performance Delta Integrale model, along with the fact that the marque would return to the UK market. The return to the UK is in part to celebrate Lancia's centenary. The world première of the new HPE concept was held at the 63rd Venice International Film Festival.

Lancia have confirmed the launch of the production version of the new Lancia Delta mid 2008 , and the car will be first unveiled at the 2008 Geneva motor show.

Delta as well as being an historical name from Lancia's past is also being interpreted this time around by Lancia as a mathematical symbol that stands for change, difference and evolution. Designed by the Lancia Style Centre, this car is aimed at the luxury end of the small sports car segment. The Delta is 4.5 metres (177.2 in) long, 1.8 metres (70.9 in) wide and 1.5 metres (59.1 in) high, and has a wheelbase of 2.7 metres (106.3 in), 10 centimetres (3.9 in) more than the Fiat Bravo.

The new Delta will offer a number of options and equipment including a Bose Hi-Fi radio incorporating a CD player and MP3 file reader with steering-wheel mounted controls, the Blue&Me system developed with Microsoft, and a brand new satellite navigation system developed with Magneti Marelli.

Further technical equipment included to effect the ride and handling will include an advanced ESC (Electronic Stability Control) system and SDC suspension (with electronic damping control).

The new Delta has also a driving assistant that gives more safety, an electric eye monitors the road and gives feedback to steering wheel to suggest corrections to the driver. The car is available also with semi-automatic parking assistant.

The Lotus Exige (pronounced: ex-seej) is a two-door, two-seat sports car made by Lotus Cars. It is essentially a coupe version of the Lotus Elise, which is a roadster.

The original Exige (NA or naturally aspirated Exige) was launched in 2000 and had a 1.8 L Rover K Series engine. It produced 170 bhp in standard form and 190 bhp (142 kW) in the VHPD version. Compared to the Elise, it had wider wheel arches, a front splitter, a large rear spoiler and a fiberglass roof.

In 2004, the Series 2 Exige was introduced. It features a 1.8 L 16-valve DOHC Toyota/Yamaha engine that produces 190 bhp with the Toyota engine designation of 2ZZ-GE. Compared to the Series 2 Elise, it has a front splitter, fiberglass hardtop roof with roof scoop, rear engine cover, and rear spoiler. The sole purpose of these aerodynamic additions to the base Elise is to create more downforce (almost 100 lb of downforce at 100 mph (160 km/h) in the Exige versus 13 lb at 100 mph (160 km/h) in the Elise).

In February 2005, Lotus announced a limited production run of 50 Exiges, using the Toyota engine with a supercharger, that increases the power output to 243 bhp. These vehicles were only available in yellow or black, representing the colors of Lotus Sport, and are badged 240R. They have a projected 0-60 mph (0-100 km/h) time of 3.9 seconds and 0-100 mph (0-160 km/h) of 9.9 seconds, with a top speed of 155 mph (249 km/h) at a cost of £44,000.00.

The North American Exige was unveiled at the Los Angeles Auto Show in January 2006. In February 2006, Lotus announced the Exige S model which used a supercharged Toyota engine producing 220 bhp. The S was also made available in North American markets as a 2007 model.

For 2008, the Exige S will have a 240bhp option and will be sold alongside the regular Exige S (220hp). The package includes upgraded AP racing brakes from the Exige Cup 240 and a larger roof scoop from the Exige Cup 255. 0-60mph (0-97km/h) is trimmed to under 4 seconds with this option. The 2008 USA Exige S 220 will feature a non-intercooled supercharger identical to the Elise SC. The 2008 UK Exige S 220 and the 2008 Exige S 240 will retain the intercooler for the supercharger.

The RX-8 was designed as a front mid-mounted, rear-wheel drive 2+2 coupé. The car has a near 50:50 weight distribution, achieved by mounting the engine behind the front axle and the fuel tank ahead of the rear axle. Weight is trimmed through the use of materials such as aluminium (hood & rear doors), and a carbon fiber composite driveshaft on the manual gearbox car; designed to reduce rotational mass (Moment of Inertia) connected to the engine. The rest of the body is steel, save for the plastic front and rear bumpers.

The car features a pair of rear-hinged "freestyle" doors (similar to suicide doors) in order to provide easier access to the rear seats. The RX-8 has no B-pillar between the front and rear doors, with the leading edge of the rear door acting as a "virtual pillar" to maintain structural rigidity. Because of the overlapping design, the rear doors can only be opened when the front doors are open.

The First Version of the RX-8, the SE, produced from Model Years 2004 to 2008, is powered by the 13B-MSP Renesis rotary engine displacing 1.3 litres (twin 654cc rotors) which, when coupled with a six speed manual transmission will typically produce 237 hp (177 kW) at 8200rpm and 211Nm (ECE) of torque at 5500 rpm. The Renesis Multi Side Port engine shows greatly improved fuel efficiency and emission improvement over the RX-7's engine.

The new revision of the Mazda RX-8 debuted at the 2008 Detroit Motor Show, with production model year starting in 2009. Additionally some minor cosmetic changes have been made most notable in the front fascia, fenders, and tail lights. No changes to the engines power output have been made, though the manual transmission models will see a lower final drive ratio of 4.777 from the previous standard of 4.444. As of October 2006 the RX-8 has won at least 37 international motoring awards including 2003 International Engine of the Year, the 2003 Japanese Car of the Year, Australia's Wheels magazine's Car of the Year for 2003, the 2004 Singapore Car of the Year, the 2004 U.S. Best Sports Car, and several UK Best Car Awards. It was named on Car and Driver magazine's Ten Best list for 2004, 2005, and 2006. Winner of the 2006-2007 Golden Icon Award (presented by Travolta Family Entertainment) for "Best Sports Car".

MERCEDES *CLC*

The Mercedes-Benz CLC-Class (codename CL203) is a luxury compact car to be produced by the Mercedes Car Group division of Daimler AG from 2008. The car is a three-door liftback. The first generation was based on the W203 C-Class and sold as the C-Class Sportcoupé or Sport Coupe. It was designed to counter the BMW Compact, though both the Sportcoupé and Compact prove unpopular with the younger buyers it was targeted towards, due to high prices compared to the lower entry-level models it was competing against, and unfavorable exchange rates. Although removed from the North American lineup in 2005, it continued on sale in other markets. From October 2000 until 2007, a total of 230,000 Sportcoupés were built in the Bremen factory and in Brazil. In Canada, it was replaced by the Mercedes-Benz B-Class.

At the launch of the Sportcoupé, a new family of supercharged four cylinder engines, dubbed M271, also debuted for the entire range C-Class range. All of them used the same 1.8 L engine, with different designations according to horsepower levels, including a version powered by natural gas. The 193 PS(142 kW/190 hp) C 230K was initially available only in the Sportcoupé.

The Sportcoupé was eventually spun off into its own separate line called the CLC-Class, but it still based on the W203 platform, with an updated front and tail inspired by the next generation W204 C-Class. Mercedes found that the Sportcoupé was a popular first Mercedes for new customers, 40 per cent of whom reportedly return to buy more expensive models later on.

The CLC is produced in Brazil at the company's plant in Juiz de Fora, close to the state border with Rio de Janeiro. The car was presented at the 2008 Mercedes-Benz Fashion Week Berlin, which took place from the 27th to 31st of January 2008.

MERCEDES *SL*

The Mercedes-Benz SL is a roadster manufactured by Mercedes since 1954. The designation SL derives from the German Sport Leicht, or Sport Light — and was first applied to the 300SL 'Gullwing' named also after its "gullwing" or upward-opening doors.

The term SL-Class refers to the marketing variations of the vehicle, including the numerous engine configurations spanning five design generations.

The 300SL roadster succeeded the Gullwing in 1957. The 4-cylinder 190SL was more widely produced with 25,881 units, starting in 1955. Cars of the open SL-Class were available as a coupe with a removable hardtop or as a roadster with convertible soft top or with both tops. Production for the 190SL and 300SL ended in 1963.

Next came the SL-Class 230SL, a new design with a low waistline and big curved greenhouse windows, and a Coupe Roadster whose distinctive roofline earned the nickname "pagoda top." Around 1968 the engine received a displacement increase and the model became known as the 250SL. The last two years of production as the 280SL saw minor changes to switch knobs, and wheel trim rings became full hubcaps.

The 1989 Mercedes SL base model was the 228 hp (170 kW) 3.0 L inline 6 300SL version. But it was the 322 hp (240 kW) 500SL (known as the 560 SL in USA) (with a 5.0 L V8 engine) which made the most headlines. The specification was high, with electric windows, mirrors, seats and roof.

1994 saw a mild facelift for the SL, and the 300SL was replaced in Europe by the SL280 and SL320 (with 2.8 L and 3.2 L I6 engines). The SL500 continued with the same powerful engine. A 389 hp (290 kW) 6.0 L V12 SL600 topped the range in 1993.

The SL320 replaced the 300SL in the United States in 1995, but the SL280 was not offered. The 6-cylinder SLs were dropped from the US lineup in 1998, leaving just the V8 and V12. The SL500 got a new 302 hp (225 kW) 5.0 L V8 for 1999.

The Facelifted 2008 SL model was revealed in the Geneva Motor Show in March. The 2008 SL gets a new front end reflecting Merc's new design philosophy, with a pair of long powerdomes on the bonnet and a single-bar grille replacing the old three-bar effort. Also improvements have been made on the engines as the 3.5L V6 is uprated to 311 PS at 6500 rpm. Compared to the previous 3.5-litre engine, the output has been boosted by 16 percent. Torque has also been improved adding 10Nm to the previous 350Nm making it 360Nm. this engine now can rev up to a max of 7200 rpm for a period as the oil temperature and other engine parameters permitting, a higher compression ratio, a new intake manifold and extensively modifying and lightening the valve train. In this case, however, the extra power does not come at the expense of fuel economy: with a consumption figure of 9.9 litres per 100 kilometres, the new SL 350 undercuts the previous model developing 200 kW by 0.4 litres per 100 kilometres.

Between 1969 and 1974, and again between 1989 and 2002, Nissan produced a high performance version of its Skyline range, called the Nissan Skyline GT-R. This car proved to be iconic for Nissan and achieved much fame and success on road and track. The Nissan GT-R, although no longer carrying the "Skyline" badge, has heritage in the Nissan Skyline GT-R. Like the Skyline GT-Rs R32 through R34, the Nissan GT-R is All-Wheel Drive with a twin-turbo 6 cylinder engine; however, the evolutionary, incremental changes between Skyline models R32 through R34 have been done away with. The four-wheel-steering HICAS system has been done away with, plus the traditional straight-6 RB26DETT engine has been replaced with a new V6 VR38DETT. Because of the GT-R's heritage, the chassis code for the all-new version has been called CBA-R35, or 'R35' for short, carrying on the naming trend from the R34 Skyline GT-R.

Two concept vehicles were displayed at motor shows prior to the unveiling of the production model. The first concept was shown at the Tokyo Motor Show in 2001 to preview what a 21st century GT-R would look like.. At the 2005 Tokyo Motor Show, Nissan unveiled a redesigned concept, the GT-R Proto, stating that the production GT-R would be 80-90% based on this concept.

The production version of the GT-R has debuted at the 2007 Tokyo Motor Show, with its launch in the Japanese market scheduled for 6 December 2007. The U.S. launch will follow in June 2008, and Canadian launch will follow in July 2008. Europe will be the third market, where it is expected to be launched late 2008. The large time distance between these releases is due to Nissan having to build GT-R performance centres where the car is built and serviced. Also the engine and rear-mounted dual-clutch gearbox are built by hand, limiting production to around 1000 cars a month. US Prices start at $66,675 for the base model.

The Nissan GT-R is powered by the VR38DETT engine, a 3.8 L DOHC V6. Two parallel Ishikawajima-Harima Heavy Industries (IHI) turbochargers provide forced induction.. Production vehicles produce at least 480 PS (473 hp/353 kW) @ 6400 rpm and 588 N·m (434 ft·lbf) @ 3200-5200 rpm. According to independent dynanometer tests, the GT-R produces 416 hp (310 kW) to 475 hp (354 kW) and 414 to 457 ft·lbf (620 N·m) of torque at the wheels. The engine also meets California ULEV (Ultra Low Emissions Vehicle) standards. A curb weight of 1740 kg (3836 lb) or 1750 kg (3858 lb) with side curtain airbags is achieved using a jig welded steel chassis with aluminum used for the hood, trunk and doors. A rear mounted 6 speed dual clutch semi-automatic transmission is used in conjunction with the ATTESA E-TS system to provide power to all four wheels and along with Nissan's Vehicle Dynamics Control (VDC-R) aids in handling and stability. Three shift modes can also be selected for various conditions.

The Peugeot 407 is a large family car produced by the French automaker Peugeot since 2004. It is available in saloon, coupé and estate variants, with both Diesel and petrol engines. The petrol engines range from 1.8 to 3.0-litres displacement, whereas the diesels are 1.6, 2.0, 2.2 and 2.7-litre V6.

The 407 was the successor to the hugely successful Peugeot 406, and was launched on May 27 2004. The streamlined design of the car was seen as quite radical, its most distinctive features being its large front grille and the steeply raked screen pillars.

The estate, known as the 407 SW, was launched four months after the saloon, whereas the coupé has been on sale since early 2006.

The saloon version of the 407 was firstly previewed with the name "407 Elixir" at the 2003 Frankfurt Motor Show. The "407 Silhouette" is a race car with most design features of the current coupé. A version almost identical to the released coupé was presented at the 2005 Geneva Motor Show under the name "407 Prologue".

The "407 Macarena" is a four-door coupé convertible produced by Heuliez and presented a at the 2006 Geneva Motor Show.

The Porsche Boxster is a mid-engined roadster built by Porsche. The Boxster is Porsche's first vehicle designed by Raymond Barth from the beginning as a roadster; all previous Porsche convertibles were based on hardtop coupes.

The first-generation Boxster (the 986) was introduced in late 1996 as a 1997 model; it was powered by a 2.5 litre flat six-cylinder engine. In 2000, the new Boxster S variant was introduced with a larger 3.2 litre motor, and the base model received a more powerful 2.7 litre engine. In 2003, styling and engine output was upgraded on both variants.

In 2005, further updates were substantial enough that Porsche internally identified the Boxster as a new 987 model. The 987s were more powerful than the 986s; engine output increased yet further in 2007, when both Boxster models received the motors from the corresponding Porsche Cayman variants.

Production of the 986 began at the former Porsche 928 facility in Stuttgart, Germany in 1996. Valmet Automotive Oy also manufactures Boxsters under contract to Porsche at a facility in Uusikaupunki, Finland. The Boxster was Porsche's biggest volume seller from its introduction in model year 1997 until the company introduced the Cayenne utility vehicle in model year 2003.

The Boxster's name is a combination of the word "boxer", referring to the vehicle's horizontally-opposed or "boxer" engine, and the word "roadster", referring to the vehicle's convertible top.

The second generation of the Boxster (internally known as the 987) made its debut at the 2004 Paris Motor Show alongside the new 911 (997). The car became available for model year 2005.

In appearance the car remains very similar to the previous generation. The most obvious styling change is to the headlights, which now have a profile similar to those of the Carrera GT, Porsche's mid-engined supercar. The intake vents on the sides of the Boxster are now larger, with more pronounced horizontal slats and are coloured metallic silver, irrespective of the paint colour on the rest of the car. The wheel arches have been enlarged to allow wheels up to 19 inches in diameter, a first for the Boxster series. The most significant updates from the 986 series are in the interior, with a more prominent circular theme evident in the instrument cluster and cooling vents. Porsche claims that the 987 Boxster shares only 20% of its components with its predecessor, despite their being almost identical from the outside. The base engine is a 2.7 L 176 kW (240 hp) flat-6, with the Boxster S getting a 3.2 L 206 kW (280 hp) engine. The Cayman series is derived from the 987.

The 986 Boxster has been on the market with virtually the same clothes from 1997-2004. The 2005 model (987) brought minor exterior changes, a completely new and improved interior and suspension as well as the typical bump in HP and torque.

The Porsche 911 (pronounced as nine eleven, neun elfer in German) is a sports car made by Porsche AG of Stuttgart, Germany. The famous, distinctive, and durable design has undergone continuous development since its introduction in autumn 1963. Mechanically it is notable for being rear engined and, until the introduction of the all-new Type 996 in 1998, air-cooled.

Since its inception the 911 has been modified, both by private teams and the factory itself, for racing, rallying and other types of automotive competition. It is often cited as the most successful competition car ever, especially when its variations are included, mainly the powerful 935.

In the international poll for the award of Car of the Century, the 911 came fifth after the Ford Model T, the Mini, the Citroën DS and the Volkswagen Beetle. It is the most successful surviving application of the air (or water) cooled opposed rear engine layout pioneered by its original ancestor, the Volkswagen Beetle.

911 Turbo meets the highest expectations in terms of engine performance. The classic flat-six unit develops 353 kW (480 hp) at 6,000 rpm from a 3.6-litre displacement. Maximum torque of 620 Nm is available between 1,950 and 5,000 rpm. To achieve that capability, we've combined VarioCam Plus with twin turbocharger units featuring Variable Turbine Geometry (VTG) – a totally new technology on a petrol-engined car. With a standard manual gearbox, the 911 Turbo requires just 3.9 seconds to reach 100 km/h (62 mph). Equipped with the latest optional Tiptronic S transmission, the car is 0.2 seconds quicker on the standard sprint. Benchmark times to 200 km/h (124 mph) are 12.8 and 12.2 seconds, respectively. Maximum speed with either transmission is 310 km/h (193 mph).

The Audi A8 is a full-size executive car built by the German automaker Audi to replace the V8 model as its flagship offering. First brought to the market in 1994, most versions of the A8 have featured quattro all-wheel-drive as standard as well as a Multitronic or Tiptronic automatic transmission. Two generations of the A8 have been produced in both short and long wheelbase form.

The second-generation A8 built on Audi's D3 platform was introduced in early 2003. The model was longer than the previous generation, with room for four or five large adult occupants in the cabin depending on rear seat configuration.

Two body variants of the second generation A8 are offered, the A8 and the long-wheelbase A8L. The A8L adds five inches of rear legroom.

Audi restyled the D3 platform A8 range slightly in 2005, endowing all variants with a taller, wider single-frame grille inspired by that of the Nuvolari concept car. The top-of-the-line 12-cylinder W12 version was the first model to be equipped with this grille; V8 models were outfitted with the new grille the following year. In addition to the styling update, new engines became available to European and Asian market customers. The entry-level 3.0 L V6 was replaced with a new 3.2 L unit featuring FSI, which it shares with the new A4.

The second-generation A8 introduced the 4.2 L Diesel V8 engine. Generating 240 kW (326 PS/322 bhp) of power, this is the most powerful diesel engine Audi has ever offered in a passenger automobile before the debut of Audi's 6.0L V12 in the Audi Q7. The engine uses two turbochargers and two intercoolers, with each turbocharger functioning exclusively for one bank of four cylinders. The 2.8L V6 FSI, which is recently added to the A8 range, has a class leading 199g/km of CO_2 emission.

For MY 2008, the A8 received new electronic safety systems. "Audi Side Assist" detects cars in the A8's blind spots. "Audi Lane Assist" helps when the driver attempts to change lanes without signaling first.

In 1998, Audi introduced the S8 variant in the vein of Mercedes-Benz AMG models. Although it shared the standard model's platform, it featured a re-tuned, 360 PS (265 kW) version of the standard V8 engine, a re-tuned suspension with larger wheels and upgraded tires, enlarged brakes and a re-calibrated version of the 5-speed Tiptronic transmission (European-spec. models had a 6-speed manual transmission option); quattro was standard. Production of the first-generation S8 ended in 2003, shortly before the introduction of the D3-platform A8.

In the last quarter of 2005, Audi introduced the second-generation S8, powered by a 450 PS (331 kW) V10 engine derived from the 5.2 L V10 used in the Lamborghini Gallardo.

The Bentley Brooklands was a full-size luxury sedan introduced for 1992 as the marque's new flagship after the Bentley Mulsanne and Bentley Eight were discontinued. The Brooklands was replaced by the Bentley Arnage in 1998 as the Bentley flagship model. At the 2007 Geneva Auto Show, Bentley resurrected the Brooklands nameplate for a two-door, four-seat coupe to be built for the 2008 model year.

The Brooklands continued Bentley's relatively angular design theme, which was also used on contemporary Rolls-Royce vehicles, throughout the 1980s and early 1990s. The exterior design featured the classic Bentley waterfall grille as well as dual headlights with wrap-around parking lights. As in many Bentley and Rolls-Royce vehicles the Brooklands also featured the trademark descending bootlid and chrome B-pillars.

The interior remained relatively unchanged from previous Bentley models with a more curvaceous design elements surrounding the leather wrapped centre console. The steering wheel and interior door panels remained unchanged. The interior continued to be surrounded by ample woodgrain which featured engraved, lighter-colored outlines on the door panels. In the U.S. prices for the Brooklands started at around $156,500.

The Bentley Brooklands Coupé will be hand-assembled, employing traditional coach-building techniques and the craftsmanship skills in wood veneer and leather hide for which Bentley is renowned. To ensure exclusivity, lifetime production will be strictly limited to 550 cars, with deliveries expected to start in the first half of 2008.

The Brooklands is powered by a twin-turbocharged 6.75-litre V8 engine producing 530 bhp (395 kW) and 1050 Nm (774 ft·lbf). It can achieve 0-60 mph in around 5 seconds, and a top speed in the region of 296 km/h (184 mph). With an optional ceramic braking system and 14 inch rotors the new Brooklands offers more stopping power than any passenger vehicle currently available for purchase.

The current 300 is a full-size sport/luxury sedan which was first shown at the 2003 New York Auto Show as a concept car and first introduced in the spring of 2004 as an early 2005 model. Its design was clearly inspired by the 1957 Chrysler 300C, the headlights and grill being the most obvious design cues taken from its ancestor.

Designed by Ralph Gilles, the new 300 was built as a high performance, sporty sedan. The 300C is also sold in Australia, the first large Chrysler sold there since the Valiant was discontinued in 1981.

The Chrysler 300 is based on the rear-wheel drive Chrysler LX platform which features components derived from the discontinued W210 Mercedes-Benz E-Class of 1996 to 2002. Such components include the suspension design, front seat frames, wiring harnesses, steering column, the 5-speed automatic's design, and a derivative of the 4-Matic all-wheel drive system. Some European versions will get a four-wheel drive version; the UK will probably not.

The basic 300 comes with standard 17-inch wheels with wheel covers, four-wheel disc brakes, traction control, and a four-speed automatic transmission. It uses a 2.7 L EER V6 making 190 hp (142 kW). In Canada, it comes standard with the Touring model's 3.5 L V6 engine. The basic 300 model was renamed to LX for 2008.

The Touring model uses a 3.5 L V6, producing 250 hp (186 kW) and 250 ft·lbf (339 N·m) of torque. It also uses a 4-speed automatic transmission, but comes with 17-inch aluminum wheels, AM/FM radio with CD player and auxiliary audio jack, Electronic Stability Program (ESP), remote keyless entry, leather trimmed seats and SIRIUS satellite radio.

The Limited model uses the Touring model's 3.5 L V6 engine, which generates 250 hp (190 kW) and 250 ft·lbf (340 N·m). Additional features include 18 inch aluminum chrome-clad wheels and Chrysler's Dual-Zone Climate Control.

The top-line 300C version uses a 5.7 L Hemi V8. This engine can run on four cylinders when less power is needed to reduce fuel consumption. The EPA has rated the 300C as getting 15 mpg–U.S. (15.68 L/100 km / 18 mpg–imp) city, 23 mpg–U.S. (10.23 L/100 km / 27.6 mpg–imp) highway. When all 8 cylinders are needed, the 300C can make 340 hp (250 kW) and 390 ft·lbf (530 N·m) torque. It uses a 5-speed automatic transmission and comes standard with 18 inch chrome-clad alloy wheels, Chrysler's "MyGIG" Infotainment System in 2008 and SIRIUS Satellite Radio and "Backseat Television" in 2008. The Chrysler 300C is unique because of the HEMI engine. This is the only HEMI that has a pushrod induction tube, located on the side of the engine. This tube is a way to make the 300C more fuel efficient and quicker, because of the air being "pulled and pushed" into the engine's induction area.

JAGUAR *XF*

The Jaguar XF is a mid-size luxury car / sports sedan made by Jaguar Cars. It was launched in the UK in 2008 and replaced the S-Type in the company's lineup. The production version of the XF debuted at the 2007 Frankfurt Motor Show, and customer deliveries commenced in March 2008.

The XF has been developed at Jaguar's Whitley design and development HQ in Coventry, UK and is built in Castle Bromwich, Birmingham, UK.

The styling of the finalised production XF varies from that of the C-XF only in a few small areas, most notably around front lights and nose, which incorporates an oval mesh grille harking back to the original XJ of 1968 and is destined to be a feature of future Jaguars. The boot lid has retained the S-Type's chromed blade to its edge, but now sports a "leaper" as well. Boot space and practicality is much improved over its predecessor, with the option of carrying a puncture repair kit instead of a spare wheel to create further space. The basic sub-structure of the XF has been carried over from the S-Type, although the body has been stretched to meet crash safety requirements, and heightened to provide additional headroom while still retaining the "saloon within a coupé" proportions. The suspension and mountings are the same as that used on the XK, while the engine line-up is basically as that used in the S-Type, utilising the Ford V8, although the supercharged SV8 model is fitted with the XK's 420 bhp unit instead of the 400 bhp standard version. Sound and vibration insulation is provided by the addition of a special underbody tray and engine mounts, a tuned exhaust system, and a double bulkhead between the engine bay and passenger compartment. There is no manual transmission option, but its six-speed automatic gearbox has been programmed to shift 10% quicker than before, and can be manually selected using paddles behind the steering wheel. The normal drive selector lever has been replaced with a rotary dial that rises from the centre console once the engine start/stop button has been pressed. Unlike its predecessor, the XF has no cloth interior option, with even the most basic model being fully trimmed in leather to even areas that have employed plastic on previous Jaguars. Real wood veneers remain a feature, but have been joined by aluminium trim to create a modern look to the passenger compartment. Another departure from the traditional Jaguar cabin ambiance is the use of pale-blue backlighting to the instruments, switchgear, and around major control panels. Some minor systems, such as the interior lighting, are controlled simply by touching the plastic light covers. The glove compartment also open to the touch.

JAGUAR *XJ*

The Jaguar XJ is a luxury saloon sold under the British Jaguar luxury marque. The XJ was launched in 1968 and has served as the Jaguar flagship model for most of its production span which continues through to today. The original model was the last Jaguar saloon to have had the input of Sir William Lyons, the company's founder.

September 1997 saw the "Mark 2" XJ revised for a final time, and this time the car (known as X308) had changed more over the X300 than the X300 had done over the XJ40. The exterior styling was mildly revised, the only real notable changes being new, shallower grille, bumpers incorporating oval front indicators & side reflectors with 1/4 chrome trims instead of the full width ones of the X300, as well as revised clear indicator rear light clusers and the fitting of modern clear lens projector headlamps.

The biggest changes lay under the bonnet and inside. An all-new, and hugely praised, V8 engine was introduced and was available in 3.2 L, 4.0 L and 4.0 L supercharged versions. The new 8-cylinder engines, built in Bridgend, Wales, not only saw the temporary end of 6-cylinder and 12-cylinder power in an XJ, but the legendary XJ6 moniker was dropped(but later re-introduced in the 2003 X350; the cars with naturally-aspirated engines were now called XJ8. The new performance figures were 290 bhp (216 kW) and 240 bhp (179 kW) for the naturally-aspirated 4.0 L and 3.2 L versions respectively and 370 bhp (276 kW) with 525 N·m (387 ft·lbf) of torque for the supercharged version.

The interior was changed greatly, featuring an all-new "oval design" dashboard (first seen in the XK) with matching door veneers. However, the basic car was now 12 years old and some now considered the limited legroom for rear passengers (except, of course, in the long-wheelbase model), which was an issue back in 1986, to now be a real Achilles' heel, especially when compared to competing models from BMW and Mercedes-Benz. Nonetheless, many overlooked this issue, citing the continued "Jaguarness" and "Britishness" of the new interior as a preferable place to spend time when compared to rivals, with the abundance of wood, chrome and leather that is a British luxury car trademark. However, for those who considered rear legroom to be a very real issue, there were LWB (long-wheelbase) versions available (and, at the very top of the range, the supercharged Daimler, known as the Super V8 in the UK & the Vanden Plas in the United States complete with fluted boot plynth & grille top, as well as full "autolux" leather interior trimming, extra highly figured walnut trim and rear picnic tables inside).

The XJR-version featured an 5 speed automatic transmission W5A580 from the Mercedes-Benz AMG E55 and other high power Benz models.

The Lexus IS-F is a high performance version of the Lexus IS series of sport luxury cars. It is the first vehicle in the F-marque line of performance vehicles from Lexus, the luxury division of Toyota. The first generation IS-F, which premiered at the 2007 North American International Auto Show, features a larger, more powerful engine than standard IS models, improved suspension and brakes, body design enhancements, and other vehicle changes. The IS-F sports 0-100 km/h (0-62 mph) acceleration in 4.6 seconds. The vehicle went on sale for late 2007 in Japan, in early 2008 in the United States, and in Europe in 2008.

In 2006, several automotive publications reported on rumors of a higher performance variant of the IS being tested at various stages of development. Spy photos of such a vehicle being tested in Germany and California were published in several magazines and websites. Among these spy reports, several photos were shown of a heavily modified and camouflaged IS sedan at the Nürburgring test track in Germany along with other disguised Lexus test vehicles. The previous generation IS 430 prototype vehicle was indicative of future possibilities for the IS series, including the likelihood that a second generation high-performance IS model could come equipped with a V8 engine. It was rumored that there would be a coupe and a convertible version for a 2009 model, as well as a convertible version of the V8-powered IS.

On 6 December 2006, Lexus officially confirmed the existence of the vehicle which they called IS-F in the press release. At the North American International Auto Show on January 8, 2007, the new IS-F was debuted to the public. The vehicle features a 5.0 L direct-injected V8 producing 416 SAE hp (423 PS, 311 kW) at 6,600 rpm, while peak torque is 371 ft·lbf (503 N·m) at 5,200 rpm. The engine also features a two-stage intake system, engine oil and automatic transmission fluid coolers and an oil pump designed for high-speed cornering. Images were leaked a couple of hours before the official announcement. At its press debut, Lexus revealed that a separate "skunk works" team designed the IS-F in a manner distinct from typical Lexus engineering efforts. The chief designer of the IS-F, Yukihiko Yaguchi, previously worked on the Toyota Supra.

The Lexus IS-F features an 8-speed automatic transmission with sequential shift (Sport Direct Shift, or SPDS), a new sport version of Lexus' electronic stability control system (Vehicle Dynamics Integrated Management, or VDIM, featuring three distinct on-off modes), and was equipped with Brembo brakes stamped with the Lexus emblem. Other design features included a four-passenger cabin with carbon-fiber panels, steering wheel paddle shifters, and 19-inch BBS forged aluminum alloy wheels. The vehicle body was lowered by 1 cm (0.5 inches) compared to the standard IS. Noticeable about the IS-F's design are its faux quad exhaust tailpipes comprised of vertically stacked dual exhaust pipes not connected to its tips on the left and right rear. For 2008, the IS-F carried a base price of $56,000 USD.

The Lexus LS is a full-size luxury sedan that serves as the flagship of Lexus, the luxury division of Toyota. Since Lexus' debut, four generations of the V8-powered, rear-wheel drive Lexus LS have been produced. The original LS 400, the first Lexus to be developed, premiered in 1989. Subsequent generations of the Lexus flagship added technological features, luxury appointments, and safety innovations. The Lexus LS is recognized as one of the most reliable vehicles ever built, and its cabin is regarded among the quietest of luxury automobiles. Each successive Lexus LS design has become the best-selling prestige luxury sedan in the United States.

In 2006, Lexus launched the fourth generation LS Series, offering the first long wheelbase version of the Lexus flagship. Beginning with the 2008 model year, an all-wheel drive hybrid joined the line up. The new LS also introduces the latest in Lexus technology, including the first production eight-speed automatic transmission and an automatic parking system. Several different Lexus LS models are sold worldwide, including standard, long wheelbase, and hybrid versions. In its largest market, the United States, starting prices for the 2008 Lexus LS range from $61,500 for the standard wheelbase LS 460 to over $104,000 for the newly produced hybrid LS 600h L, which is pushed into ultra-luxury category because of its six figure price.

Lexus' flagship model has held the highest ranking in J.D. Power's Vehicle Dependability Survey for over twelve consecutive years, and Consumer Reports has named the LS as the most dependable vehicle ever tested. In 2007, international jurors named the LS 460 as the World Car of the Year.

Lexus introduced the LS 600h L (UVF46), the world's first V8-powered full hybrid, at the 2006 New York Auto Show. The long wheelbase LS 600h L is equipped with Lexus Hybrid Drive, featuring a 5.0 L 2UR-FSXE V8 engine mated to a high-output electric motor with nickel-metal hydride battery packs. This system generates an output of 438 hp (327 kW), comparable to V12 sedans such as the BMW 760Li (which also produces 438 hp), but the systems total potential power output is 610hp. The LS hybrid features all-wheel drive with a Torsen limited-slip differential, is equipped with a two-stage continuously variable transmission (CVT) along with the Adaptive Variable Air Suspension, and achieves an environmentally-friendly Super Ultra Low Emission Vehicle (SULEV) rating. The 600h L mileage, at 20 mpg city, 22 highway, and 21 combined, is slightly higher overall than the lower-powered non-hybrid 460 L's 16/24/19 mpg numbers (these are EPA 2008 model-year figures). In Europe, the LS 600h has been rated at 9.5 L/100 km (24.8 mpg U.S.), the LS 460 at 11.1 L/100 km (21.2 mpg U.S.). The transmission features a three-mode power switch for control of torque output between hybrid (normal), power, or snow modes; an additional EV mode allows for ultra-quiet driving under full electric power.

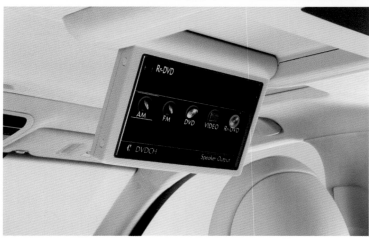

MAYBACH *62 Landaulet*

The Maybach 62 Landaulet, based on the Maybach 62S, revives the classic landaulet car body style, which was popular in the 1920s and 30s. Powered by the 62S's 612 horsepower (456 kW) biturbo V12, the Landaulet's front seats are fully enclosed and separated from the rear passenger compartment by a power divider window. Back seat passengers get a sliding soft roof that lets them take in the sun from the comfort of the back seats. The chauffeur's area is finished in black leather, while the rear is done in all white with piano black and gold-flecked black granite inserts. Also, the opacity of the glass partition separating the driver from the passengers can be electronically controlled.

Maybach publicly unveiled the Landaulet at the Middle East International Auto Show around the end of November 2007 as a concept car. It has recently been confirmed that the car will go into limited production .

MERCEDES *CL500*

The Mercedes-Benz CL-Class is a full-sized grand tourer produced by the German automaker Mercedes-Benz, which stands for Comfort Leicht in German, or Comfort Light in English. Originally derived from the SL-Class roadster, it has since been based on the S-Class sedan. Known at first as the SEC and later S coupe, it was spun off into its own line and current name in 1998. The CL continues to follow the same development cycle as the S, though riding on a slightly shorter wheelbase and offering smaller selection of engines, mostly tending towards the high-powered of the range.

The closest competitor was the now-discontinued BMW 8 Series coupe. However, while the performance-oriented 8 series had a cramped 2+2 seating arrangement, the rear passenger volume of the CL and its previous incarnations is large enough to classify them as 2-door sedans by the SAE, making the CL one of the few full-sized coupes that offer a combination of engine power and luxury accommodation.

The present generation of the CL-Class, or C216, is currently available in four models: CL500 (CL550 in America), CL600, CL63 AMG and CL65 AMG. The 2008 price ranges from $103,875 to $197,775. The most powerful model of the CL is the most expensive Mercedes-branded vehicle (with the exception of the SLR and the S Class Pullman), slightly edging out its equivalent in the flagship S-Class.

The new model was officially unveiled at the end of June 2006 and was presented at the 2006 Paris Salon. The W216 is offered in four models, the V8-powered CL500, the high-performance V8-powered CL63 AMG and the high-end V12-powered CL600 and CL65AMG . The CL500 is sold as the CL550 in North America. The class is based on the chassis of the W221 S-Class and shares similar design cues together with the CLS-Class. The two-door coupe weighs 2185 kg (4817 lb) and like its predecessor, has no B-pillar interrupting the sleek curve of the side windows. The C216 makes use of the Distronic Plus cruise control, which debuted on the 2007 S-Class. This system is able to bring the car to a complete stop, and accelerate again to the pre-set speed, to keep a pre-set distance away from the car ahead of it. This Mercedes-Benz CL has also debuted with the new Active NightVision program that enables drivers to view the conditions in front of the car despite the dark surroundings. Mercedes has no plans to upgrade the 5.5L motor in the CL500/CL550 because it is already class leading, even with its older SOHC design.

The Rolls-Royce Phantom is a British ultra-luxury saloon automobile made by Rolls-Royce Motor Cars, in the United Kingdom. It was launched in 2003 and is the latest Rolls-Royce branded car. It has a 6.75 L, 48-valve, V12 engine that produces 453 hp (338 kW) and 531 ft·lbf (720 N·m) of torque. The engine is derived from BMW's existing V12 powerplant.

It is 1.63 m (63 in) tall, 1.99 m (74.8 in) wide, 5.83 m (228 in) long, and weighs 2485 kg (5478 lb). The body of the car is built on an aluminium space frame and the Phantom can accelerate to 100 km/h (62 mph) in 5.7 s. It has a six-speed automatic transmission and double wishbone suspension.

An extended wheelbase Phantom was presented in March 2005 at the Geneva Motor Show, which is 250 mm (9.8 in) longer than the standard Phantom. It is currently referred to as the Phantom Extended Wheelbase (or EWB).

Only 15 percent of components are sourced from BMW models such as the BMW 7 Series. This comprises the powertrain, and electronics. The Phantom uses a unique chassis platform, body, interior, and retains the traditional Rolls-Royce design cues.

The intention was to avoid being seen as just an extension to the BMW range. When DaimlerChrysler introduced its Maybach luxury saloon, it was criticized for producing "the ultimate Mercedes" instead of a totally different car. The car shared many components with and looked like the less expensive S-Class Sedan. BMW learned from this lesson, selling the Phantom through separate dealerships where BMWs are not sold, while the Maybach showroom also sells the most basic of Mercedes models.

The aluminium spaceframe body is built in a BMW plant in Dingolfing, Germany and the V12 engine in Munich. Final assembly, as well as all wood and leather work, for each customer's individual specification is at a purpose built €100M plant at Goodwood, West Sussex, England. The Goodwood plant contains only two robots to paint the spaceframe body; all other work is done by hand, in keeping with the Rolls-Royce tradition.

Rolls-Royce Phantom Drophead Coupé is the latest convertible made by Rolls-Royce which debuted at the 2007 North American International Auto Show in Detroit, Michigan on January 7, 2007. The platform is based on the Rolls-Royce Phantom and has styling heavily derived from the 100EX concept car unveiled to celebrate the company's centennial in 2004.

The Chevrolet Tahoe (and similar GMC Yukon) is a full-size SUV from General Motors. Chevrolet and GMC sold two different-sized SUVs under their Blazer/Jimmy model names through the early 1990s. This situation changed when GMC rebadged the full-size Jimmy as the Yukon in 1992. Chevrolet waited until 1994's introduction of a four-door version to rebadge the mid-size S-10 Blazer as the Blazer, renaming the full-size Blazer as the Tahoe.

The Chevrolet Tahoe and GMC Yukon currently serve as General Motors' full-size SUVs. Lengthened wheelbase models are available for both as the Suburban for the Tahoe and Yukon XL for the Yukon. A luxury Denali model joined the Yukon lineup in 1998. As of 2002, a Denali version of the Yukon XL was also available as the Yukon XL Denali.

In North America, the Tahoe is a popular alternative to the Ford Crown Victoria for police car use, especially in rural areas. General Motors replaced the Tahoe and Yukon on the new GMT900 platform in late 2005 as a 2007. A hybrid version of the Yukon, which uses the shared GM/Chrysler Advanced Hybrid System 2, is expected to follow with the 2008 models. The GMT900 based Tahoe and Yukon exceeded initial sales expectations and continue to sell well despite a weakening market for large SUVs.

For 2007 the GMC Yukon and Chevrolet Tahoe received different front fascias and hood. The GMC Yukon features a monolithic grille and headlights, while the Chevrolet Tahoe's grille is divided by a body colored bar similar to the chrome bar found on most of the GMT800 Tahoes. While the Tahoe's hood now features a design attribute obtruding from its otherwise smooth contour, the Yukon features a smooth hood with two slight curves on both sides of the hood. Both the new Yukon and Tahoe feature a more angular design that supposedly gives the vehicles a more upscale appearance. The interior was significantly redesigned as well. It features a new wooded trim dashboard with new chrome accented instrument controls. New door panels as well as new seats were also added to the interior.

Short wheelbase and police Tahoe production began at Arlington Assembly on December 1, 2005. SWB Yukon production began in early 2006, with Janesville Assembly coming on line as well. Long wheelbase versions began at Janesville and Silao Assembly in March.

Tahoe made its hybrid electric debut in fall, 2007. In January, 2008, starting price was USD$50,540. Black 2008 GMC Yukon Hybrids have replaced the GMC Yukon Denalis on CBS's hit-series CSI. However the GMC Yukon Denali XL is still being used as the CSI's mobile lab/command vehicle.

The Chevrolet Volt is a plug-in hybrid concept car created by General Motors. However, the company has avoided the use of the term "hybrid," preferring to call it an electric vehicle with a "range extender" due to its design. The vehicle is designed to run purely on electricity from on-board batteries for up to 40 miles (64 km), or about half the range of the GM EV1 — a large enough distance to cover the daily commutes of most Americans, which is around 33 miles (53 km). With use of a small internal combustion engine driving a generator to resupply the batteries, the vehicle's range is potentially increased to 640 miles (1,030 km) on the highway. General Motors Corp. had originally planned to build 60,000 of its Volt electric cars for their inaugural year, however have now scaled back production to 10,000 units.

The Volt concept vehicle was officially unveiled at the North American International Auto Show (NAIAS) on January 7, 2007 in Detroit, Michigan. An updated version was unveiled at the Shanghai Auto Show in April 2007 in Shanghai, China. At the time of unveiling, the Volt project had been in existence for less than a year. The Volt was targeted to cost around $20,000 to $30,000. As of April 2008 Lutz said that the realistic unsubsidised cost has risen to $48K. He reckons that $40,000 might be possible, without making any profit. Only government tax incentives could take the price tag nearer to $30,000.

GM faces competition from Nissan Motors, which announced its own electric car on May 13, and a bunch of startups, some backed by Silicon Valley money, angling to sell their own futuristic vehicles.

General Motors said it will have the Volt on the market in 2010. To help spur battery research, GM selected two companies to provide advanced lithium-ion batterypacks: Compact Power, which uses manganese oxide based cells made by its parent company, LG Chemical, and Continental Automotive Systems, which uses nanophosphate based cylindrical cells made by A123Systems. However, on August 9, 2007 GM established a more close-knit relationship with A123Systems so that the two companies could co-develop a Volt-specific battery cell. This cell was later unveiled at the EVS23 industry convention in Anaheim, CA. Work with CPI has continued at a rapid pace, and in late 2007 CPI delivered two fully-functional prototype battery packs to GM's testing facilities. On January 31, 2008, A123 and Continental delivered their first prototype to GM's European test facilities. GM will likely use both suppliers for the Volt, although this remains a matter of speculation.

The Ford Escape Hybrid, launched in 2004, is a gas-electric hybrid powered version of the Ford Escape SUV developed by the Ford Motor Company. Built in Kansas City, Missouri, it was the first hybrid SUV to hit the market. A similar vehicle, the Mercury Mariner Hybrid is sold by Ford's Mercury marque. A third variation, the Mazda Tribute Hybrid, is expected to arrive in the fall of 2007 as a 2008 Model Year vehicle with a limited production run for the California market.

Hybrid versions can be identified by the "Hybrid" badges on the front driver's and passenger's doors as well as on the tailgate. In addition, the driver's side window in the cargo area is smaller in size in order to accommodate a ventilation slot for the high voltage battery. There was also a "Special Appearance Package" available as an option on the 2005-2007 Hybrid models. This package replaced the traditional lower cladding of the Escape with a silver finish (see picture).

The Escape hybrid is a "full" hybrid electric system, meaning the system can switch automatically between pure electric power, pure gasoline engine power, or a combination of electric battery and gasoline engine operating together, for maximum performance and efficiency at all speeds and loads. When braking or decelerating, the Escape's hybrid system uses regenerative braking, where the electric drive motor becomes a generator, converting the vehicle's momentum back to electricity for storage in the batteries. With 155 hp (116 kW), the Hybrid Escape has nearly the same acceleration performance as the conventional 200 hp (150 kW) V6 Escape.

The Escape Hybrid uses technology similar to that used in Toyota's Prius. Ford engineers realized their technology may conflict with patents held by Toyota, which led to a 2004 patent-sharing accord between the companies, licensing Ford's use of some of Toyota's hybrid technology in exchange for Toyota's use of some of Ford's diesel and direct-injection engine technology. Both Ford and Toyota state that Ford received no technical assistance from Toyota in developing the hybrid powertrain, but that some hybrid engine technologies developed by Ford independently were found to be similar to technologies previously patented by Toyota. Aisin Seiki Co. Ltd., a Japanese automotive components supplier belonging to the Toyota Group, supplies the hybrid continuously variable transmission for the Escape Hybrid. While Toyota produces its third-generation Prius transmission in-house, Aisin is the only supplier of hybrid transmissions to other manufacturers. Friction has arisen concerning Aisin's allocation of limited production capacity and engineering resources to Ford.

The Honda FCX Clarity is a hydrogen fuel cell automobile manufactured by Honda. Currently there are more than twenty 2002 prototype-based, leased vehicles in the hands of customers in three different American states, including the state of New York, city of Las Vegas, Chula Vista, San Francisco and the South Coast Air Quality Management District.

Limited marketing of a latest fuel cell vehicle based on the 2007 concept model is to begin in 2008 in Japan and the United States. Honda believes it could start mass producing vehicles based on the FCX concept by the year 2018.

At the 2006 Detroit Auto Show, Honda announced that it would make a production version of the concept FCX it had shown at the 2005 Tokyo Motor Show. On 25 September 2006 this new version was unveiled. The updated four-door sedan version looks much sleeker and more futuristic, and has a high focus on comfort and interior space. It has a much more spacious interior with a mixture of plastic, wood and leather. Production is expected to begin in 2008 in Japan and the U.S. The production version will closely resemble the concept, although it is unknown if some of the concept's more radical features, such as a tilting instrument panel, will be included.

According to Honda, the new fuel-cell stack is 20% smaller, 30% lighter and has a higher output of 100 kW (136 PS/134 bhp) . The new powerplant is 180 kg lighter, 40% smaller in volume and has a high energy efficiency of 60%, compared with 20% for most internal combustion engines, 30% for most hybrid powerplants and 50% for the previous generation FCX.

The new powerplant utilizes three electric motors: one front-drive motor with an output of up to 80 kW, this motor's shaft is coaxial with the gearbox for a more compact front-end, and two smaller motors with a maximum output of 25 kW driving one of the rear wheels each. This layout makes the FCX technically an all-wheel-drive vehicle. The updated FCX has a maximum speed of 160 km/h (100 mph).

The new FCX utilizes several interesting new features. The new V Flow fuel cell stack can operate at temperatures as low as –30 °C. This is achieved by allowing the hydrogen to flow vertically in the fuel cell stack. The tanks can store up to 5 kg (171 litres) of hydrogen at a pressure of 350 atmospheres, thanks to the new hydrogen absorption materials used. This allows a longer range of up to 350 miles (570 km).

To support the hydrogen fuel-cell technology, Honda also introduced the Home Energy Station (HES). This home solution can convert natural gas to electricity, heat and hydrogen to refuel fuel-cell vehicles. This allows consumers to refuel vehicles with hydrogen at home, important until hydrogen stations become widespread. Alternatively, the hydrogen can be used in the HES's built-in hydrogen fuel cell, providing up to 5 kW of normal or backup electricity and/or hot water for the home.

In creating the Denki Cube, the designers started with a well-defined canvas, the current-generation Nissan Cube. The iconic Cube has always been the antithesis of traditional automotive style – square, minimalist, asymmetrical and humble – yet also warm, relaxing, practical and undeniably charming. To this solid foundation, the Denki Cube adds a new EV powertrain and unique exterior and interior treatments.

The Denki Cube exterior features fresh front and rear styling treatments, including a new "electric themed" front grille design with an AC power charging port, a radical "lightning" headlight design and new bumpers and turn signal lamps. In the rear, the signature Cube asymmetrical rear quarter area (with wraparound glass on one side) has been enhanced by a new bumper with hidden taillights. The roof sheet metal has been replaced with a full fixed glass panel that enhances the interior's sense of wide-open space. The Denki Cube exterior also features new door mirrors and unique 16-inch wheel covers. The finishing touch is provided by a special white pearl paint and graphics.

Inside, the Denki Cube reflects the designers' intention of creating a relaxing, moving social hub, like a favorite room in an owner's house. Though the production Cube offers three rows of seating, the Denki Cube offers only two rows and the wheelbase has been stretched 9.4 inches in order to better accommodate the lithium-ion battery cells. The newly designed front and second row seats are joined by a revised instrument panel with an IP-mounted shift button, a special steering wheel design and new door panel and cargo area trim.

The biggest transformation from production Cube to Denki Cube is one that isn't visible – the replacement of the standard 1.3-liter inline 4-cylinder gasoline engine with an electric motor and laminated lithium-ion batteries located under the floor and seats. The laminated structure and unique material technology offer more power, energy and battery stability, as well as compact size and packaging flexibility, versus conventional cylindrical batteries.

Nissan's compact lithium-ion battery technology, one of the company's traditional strengths, provides batteries with twice as much energy compared with a conventional cylindrical battery of the same type and safer operation due to the use of chemically stable spine-structured manganese for the electrode material. In order to better leverage Nissan's lithium-ion battery capabilities, a new company, Automotive Energy Supply Corp. (AESC), was jointly established with NEC Corp. and NEC Tokin Corp. – with the goal of dramatically enhancing future battery performance and reducing battery costs.

Hybrid
NISSAN *Pivo*

The Nissan Pivo is a concept car created by Nissan. The Pivo was first introduced at the 2005 Tokyo Motor Show. The car is essentially a 360 degree rotating cabin on a chassis of 4 wheels, and hence eliminates the need for reversing and makes parking easier.

Rather than a typical internal combustion engine, the Pivo is powered by a lithium-ion battery which emits less harmful gases into the atmosphere than other typical vehicles. The car's futuristic design incorporates large doors for easy access to the cabin and large windscreens and windows for high visibility. As well as the fully rotational cabin, the Pivo features Nissan's Around View Monitor system. This reduces blindspots (areas of the road which cannot be seen from the driver's position) by displaying the outside surroundings on screens mounted on the inside of the car's A-pillars.

While the word pivo means beer in Czech and several other Slavic languages, the car design has nothing to do with beer cans or keg barrels.

The idea behind the "Smart car" was to create a vehicle easy to park and short enough to allow "nose-in" parking. Its length of 250 centimetres (98.4 in) would equal the width of a regular parking slot, allowing two or three Smarts to park in the space as one normal car.

The project, started by Swiss watch manufacturer Swatch, was nicknamed the "Swatchmobile". The name Smart is an acronym for Swatch Mercedes ART. Intended to use innovative features (such as a hybrid engine) and be affordable for young people, the Smart had similar design objective to the Citroën 2CV of the 1940s.

Swatch CEO Nicolas Hayek sought an established car maker to produce his Swatch car. After General Motors reviewed and rejected the project as potentially unprofitable, Hayek found a partner in Volkswagen. Due to VW's own financial weakness at the time, plans never reached a final stage so Swatch teamed up with Daimler-Benz. The purpose-built factory complex Smartville in Hambach, France, was established in 1994 as a joint-venture of Daimler-Benz and Swatch. The final car design proved to be far from Hayek's expectations: its engine eco-technology was outside of Mercedes' goal. The joint venture experienced heavy losses and dispute then Swatch pulled out.

In 2005, DaimlerChrysler decided against purchasing a 50% share in the Dutch NedCar plant used to manufacture the Forfour supermini. DC also halted development on the Formore and decided to discontinue production of the Roadster.

In 2006, after dwindling sales, Smart GmbH was liquidated and its operations were absorbed within the Mercedes-Benz automobile group. It was later revealed that Smart GmbH lost nearly 4 billion euros from 2003 to 2006. In the same year, DaimlerChrysler announced that it would also cancel the Forfour and redesign the Fortwo to debut in Europe in 2007.

An electric, rechargeable version is being released in the UK, by a separate company, as a lease vehicle on a limited basis. At the Smart Car Brooklands event in July 1998, a Smart EV was on display within "MercedesWorld" and a representative stated that the car would be for sale in the UK in 2001 .

The main structure of the car is a stiff structure called a Tridion Safety Cell, which is designed to activate the crumple zones of a colliding vehicle. This design creates a very strong safety cell around the passengers. However, it also subjects them to higher forces during an accident than in a conventional car.

Smart cars have been modified by Brabus of Germany, also to house motors from powerful Japanese sport motorcycles, such as the Suzuki Hayabusa 1352 cc inline four-cylinder (Smartuki being a notable example). These cars are known as "Diablos" ("Devils" in English). The most powerful models can accelerate from 0 to 60 mph (0 to 100 km/h) in less than 3.5 seconds.

The Tesla Roadster is a fully electric sports car, and is the first car produced by electric car firm Tesla Motors. The car can travel 225 mi (362 km) on a single charge of its lithium-ion battery pack and accelerate from 0-60 mph (97 km/h) in 3.9 seconds with the development transmission. The Roadster's efficiency is reported as 133 W·h/km (4.7 mi/kW·h), equivalent to 135 mpg–U.S. (1.74 L/100 km / 162.1 mpg–imp).

The Roadster was developed with help from Lotus Cars. Lotus supplied the basic chassis development technology from its Lotus Elise, with which the Tesla engineers designed a new chassis. Barney Hatt at Lotus' design studio developed the styling with input from Tesla. Tesla's designers chose to construct the body panels using resin transfer molded carbon fiber composite to minimize weight; this choice makes the Roadster one of the least expensive cars with an entirely carbon fiber skin. The car will be assembled at the Lotus factory in Hethel, England, with drivetrain components and body components supplied to the factory by Tesla.

The Roadster shares less than 10% of its components with the Lotus Elise; shared components are confined to the windshield, air bags, tires, some dashboard parts, and suspension components. The parts supply chain extends around the world; Tesla Motor's plant in Taiwan manufactures the motors and the Energy Storage System is assembled at Tesla's plant in Thailand. Chassis are manufactured in Norway. SOTIRA, in St. Meloir & Pouancé France, create the RTM carbon fiber body panels. The Roadster's brakes and airbags are made by Siemens in Germany and crash testing was conducted at Siemens as well.

The AC motor and drivetrain technology are more advanced than versions used in the GM EV1 and AC Propulsion tzero. Tesla Motors licensed AC Propulsion's Reductive Charging patent which covers integration of the charging electronics with the inverter, thus reducing mass, complexity and cost. Tesla Motors then designed and built its own power electronics, motor, and other drivetrain components that incorporate this licensed technology from AC Propulsion.

Several prototypes of the Tesla Roadster were produced from 2004 through 2007. Initial studies were done in two "mule" vehicles. Ten Engineering Prototypes (EP1 thru EP10) were then built and tested in late 2006 and early 2007 which lead to many minor changes. Tesla then produced seventeen Validation Prototypes (VP1 thru VP17) which were delivered beginning in March, 2007. These final revisions were endurance and crash tested in preparation for series production.

In January, 2008 the NHTSA announced that it would grant a waiver of the advanced air bag rule noting that the Tesla Roadster already includes standard air bags; similar waivers have been granted to many other small volume manufacturers as well including Lotus, Ferrari and Bugatti.

In 1994, Toyota executive Takeshi Uchiyamada was given the task of creating a new car which would be both fuel efficient and environmentally friendly. The engineering team quickly settled on a hybrid engine design, but many technical and engineering problems had to be solved within the three years that the team was given to bring the car to the Japanese market, a goal they barely achieved as the first Prius went on sale in December 1997. A main problem was the longevity of the battery, which needed to be between 7 to 10 years. The solution the engineers came up with was to keep the battery pack between 60% and 40% charged, proving to be the "sweet spot" for extending the battery life to roughly that of the other car components.

Sales in Europe began at the start of 2001, by which time the car was more than three years old. The car was a modest success in Japan and after gathering several years of test data from the Japanese early adopters, the company felt it was safe to put it on sale in the U.S. market. Sales were small at first (though the waiting list was six months for the first few years in the U.S.) but picked up substantially with a complete redesign in 2004. The Prius is considered to be a successful car for Toyota from both technical and marketing perspectives. The break-even date is uncertain, but according to the head of the Prius team, the company initially lost money on the Prius.

The Prius is marketed as a fuel efficient car. In the United States, the Environmental Protection Agency (EPA) test results must be posted on new vehicle windows, and are the only fuel consumption figures that can be advertised. Similar to other vehicles, Consumer Reports viewed the initial estimate as flawed and issued their own assessment giving a real-world fuel consumption of 44 mpg–U.S. (5.35 L/100 km / 52.8 mpg–imp) for the Prius instead of 55 mpg–U.S. (4.28 L/100 km / 66.1 mpg–imp) (51 mpg–U.S. (4.61 L/100 km / 61.3 mpg–imp) highway, 60 mpg–U.S. (3.92 L/100 km / 72.1 mpg–imp) city. EPA testing procedures for all vehicles were revised in 2007. According to the EPA's revised estimates, the combined fuel consumption for the 2008 Prius is 46 mpg–U.S. (5.11 L/100 km / 55.2 mpg–imp), making it the most efficient car available in the U.S. in 2008

INDEX